The Mind's Pathway to Ultimate Peace

Enhance Your Cognitive Competencies with Mindfulness Techniques

BY

Alice J.Wilson

Table of CONTENTS

Why You Should Buy This Book

"The Mind's Pathway to Ultimate Peace"

In today's fast-paced world, stress, anxiety, and mental fatigue are common challenges. This book offers a practical and evidence-based approach to cultivating a calm and focused mind.

Here's why you should consider this book:

- **Improve Your Mental Health:** Learn effective techniques to reduce stress, anxiety, and depression.
- **Enhance Cognitive Abilities:** Boost your memory, focus, and creativity through mindfulness practices.
- **Develop Emotional Intelligence:** Cultivate self-awareness, empathy, and effective communication skills.
- **Achieve Inner Peace:** Find tranquility and contentment in your daily life.
- **Transform Your Life:** Apply mindfulness to various aspects of your life, from work to relationships.

By investing in this book, you're investing in yourself. It's a guide to a happier, healthier, and more fulfilling life.

INTRODUCTION

The Power of the Mind

The human mind, a complex and intricate organ, holds the key to unlocking our full potential. It is the source of our thoughts, emotions, and behaviors, shaping our experiences and defining our reality. By harnessing the power of our minds, we can achieve greater levels of happiness, success, and fulfillment.

The Role of Mindfulness

Mindfulness, the practice of being present in the moment, has been shown to have profound benefits for both mental and physical health. By cultivating mindfulness, we can enhance our cognitive abilities, reduce stress, and improve our overall well-being.

The Structure of the Book

This book is designed to guide you on a journey of self-discovery and personal growth. We will explore the core principles of mindfulness, practical techniques to incorporate mindfulness into your daily life, and the science behind its benefits. Through the chapters, you will learn how to:

- **Understand your mind:** Explore the workings of the human brain and the impact of thoughts and emotions.
- **Practice mindfulness:** Learn various mindfulness techniques to calm your mind and reduce stress.
- **Enhance cognitive abilities:** Improve your focus, memory, and creativity.

- **Cultivate emotional intelligence:** Develop empathy, self-awareness, and effective communication skills.
- **Integrate mindfulness into daily life:** Apply mindfulness to various aspects of your life, from work to relationships.

By the end of this book, you will have the tools and knowledge to transform your life through the power of mindfulness.

Chapter 01

Understanding the Mind

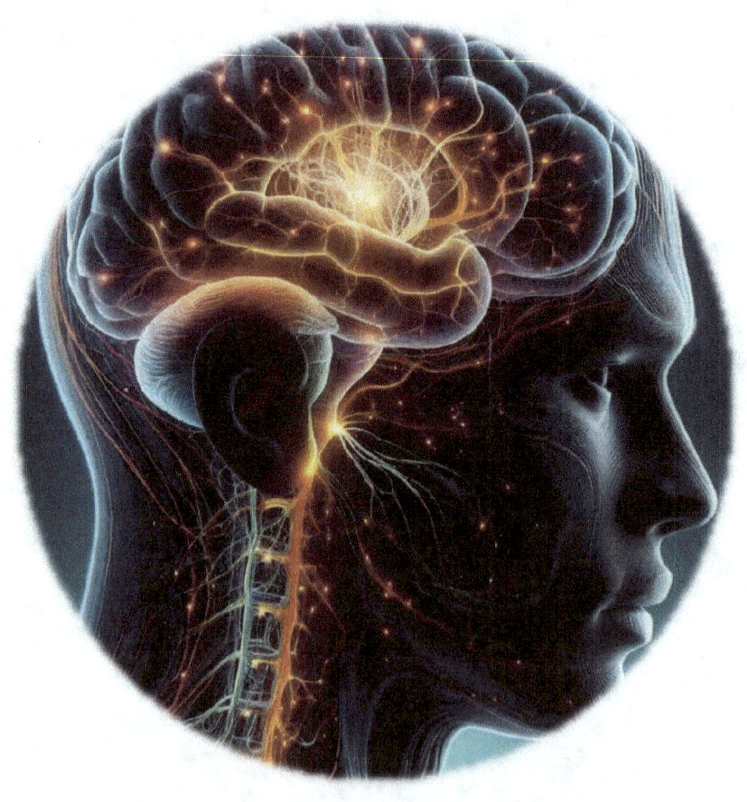

The Basics of the Human Brain

The human brain is a complex organ responsible for everything we think, feel, and do. It consists of billions of neurons that communicate with each other to create thoughts, emotions, and behaviors. These neurons form intricate networks, transmitting signals at lightning speed through synapses. The brain is divided into regions, each specializing in specific functions, such as the prefrontal cortex for decision-making, the hippocampus for memory, and the amygdala for emotions.

The brain's energy demands are immense, consuming about 20% of the body's total energy despite making up only about 2% of its weight. Proper nutrition, hydration, and sleep are critical for maintaining optimal brain function, as these factors directly impact the brain's efficiency and capacity for learning.

The Power of Neuroplasticity

One of the most exciting discoveries in neuroscience is neuroplasticity, the brain's ability to change and adapt throughout our lives. This ability allows the brain to reorganize itself by forming new neural connections in response to learning, experience, or injury. For example, when learning a new skill, like playing an instrument or solving puzzles, specific brain regions strengthen over time, reinforcing the pathways involved.

By practicing mindfulness, we can enhance neuroplasticity, strengthening neural connections and improving cognitive function. Mindfulness involves focusing on the present moment without judgment, which fosters new neural pathways that promote resilience and emotional regulation. Studies have shown that regular mindfulness practice can even lead to structural changes in the brain, such as increased gray matter density in areas associated with learning, memory, and emotional control.

The Mind-Body Connection

The mind and body are interconnected, and what affects one affects the other. Stress, anxiety, and negative emotions can have a significant impact on our physical health, contributing to issues like high blood pressure, weakened immunity, and chronic pain. Conversely, poor physical health can exacerbate mental health challenges.

Mindfulness not only helps reduce stress but also positively impacts physical health by regulating hormones like cortisol and promoting better sleep quality. Engaging in activities such as yoga or mindful breathing exercises can further strengthen this connection, as these practices harmonize mental focus with physical movement, creating a sense of balance and well-being.

The Role of Emotions in Mental Health

Emotions play a crucial role in our mental health. They are signals that provide information about our needs and environment, guiding our decisions and interactions. While it's important to acknowledge and accept our emotions, it's also essential to learn how to manage them effectively.

For instance, suppressing emotions can lead to emotional outbursts or chronic stress, whereas expressing them constructively fosters healthier relationships and self-awareness. Mindfulness can help us regulate our emotions by increasing our ability to observe them without reacting impulsively. Techniques like labeling emotions (e.g., "I feel anger" rather than "I am angry") create a psychological distance, allowing us to respond with greater clarity and wisdom.

The Impact of Stress on the Mind

Chronic stress can have a detrimental effect on our mental and physical health, impairing memory, reducing focus, and increasing the risk of anxiety and depression. Stress activates the "fight or flight" response, releasing stress hormones like adrenaline and cortisol, which can be helpful in short bursts but harmful when sustained over time.

Mindfulness helps to counteract this by activating the parasympathetic nervous system, which promotes relaxation and recovery. Simple practices such as body scans, where you mentally check in with each part of your body, or mindful walking, where you focus on the sensations of each step, can significantly reduce anxiety and improve overall focus.

Cultivating a Positive Mindset

A positive mindset is essential for overall well-being, as it influences how we perceive challenges, setbacks, and opportunities. However, cultivating positivity doesn't mean ignoring difficulties—it involves consciously choosing to focus on solutions and personal growth.

Practicing gratitude, for instance, shifts our focus from what's lacking to what we have, fostering contentment and joy. Positive affirmations can help rewire negative thought patterns, reinforcing self-belief and confidence. Visualization, another powerful tool, involves imagining desired outcomes vividly, which can boost motivation and create a mental blueprint for achieving goals. Together, these practices nurture an optimistic outlook and enhance resilience in the face of life's challenges.

Chapter 02

The Core Principles of Mindfulness

What is Mindfulness?

Mindfulness is the practice of being fully present in the moment, without judgment. It involves paying attention to your thoughts, feelings, and sensations without getting caught up in them. Mindfulness is a skill that can be cultivated through regular practice, but it's also a way of life that encourages intentional awareness and acceptance.

Mindfulness has its roots in ancient Buddhist traditions, but it has been adapted and embraced in modern psychology and wellness practices. It's not about emptying the mind of thoughts but rather about observing those thoughts and feelings with curiosity and without attaching labels of "good" or "bad."

Modern neuroscience supports the effectiveness of mindfulness, showing that regular practice can lead to changes in brain regions associated with attention, emotion regulation, and stress reduction.

The benefits of mindfulness are numerous and well-documented. Regular mindfulness practice can lead to:

- **Reduced stress and anxiety**: By focusing on the present moment, you can reduce feelings of stress and anxiety. This happens because mindfulness lowers the levels of cortisol, the stress hormone, and helps activate the relaxation response.
- **Improved focus and concentration**: Mindfulness strengthens the brain's prefrontal

cortex, enhancing your ability to focus and stay productive, even in high-pressure situations.

- **Enhanced emotional regulation**: Mindfulness increases activity in the anterior cingulate cortex, a brain region involved in controlling emotional responses, allowing you to manage emotions more effectively.
- **Increased self-awareness**: By paying attention to your thoughts and feelings, you can gain a deeper understanding of yourself. This self-awareness fosters personal growth and more authentic relationships.
- **Improved physical health**: Mindfulness can help reduce chronic pain, improve sleep quality, and boost the immune system by decreasing inflammation and promoting relaxation.

Mindfulness vs. Meditation: Understanding the Difference

While mindfulness and meditation are often used interchangeably, they are not the same thing. Meditation is a specific practice that involves focusing the mind on a particular object, such as the breath or a mantra, often in a seated and structured setting.

Mindfulness, on the other hand, is a broader concept that can be practiced at any moment during any activity. For instance, you can be mindful while eating, walking, or even cleaning. Think of meditation as one of the tools to cultivate mindfulness. Both practices complement each other and, when combined, can amplify the benefits.

The Three Pillars of Mindfulness: Mindfulness of the Body, Mind, and Emotions

Mindfulness of the Body:
This involves paying attention to the sensations in your body, such as the feeling of your breath, the weight of your body, and any physical sensations. It can help you become more attuned to your physical health and identify signs of stress or tension before they escalate.

Example Practice: A body scan meditation, where you mentally focus on each part of your body, starting from your toes and moving upward, noticing any tension or sensations.

Mindfulness of the Mind:
This involves paying attention to your thoughts without judgment. Notice your thoughts as they arise, without getting caught up in them or letting them define you. This practice fosters cognitive clarity and reduces overthinking.

Example Practice: Labeling your thoughts as "planning," "remembering," or "worrying" can create psychological distance, making it easier to let them go.

Mindfulness of Emotions:
This involves paying attention to your emotions without judgment. Observe your emotions as they arise, without becoming overwhelmed by them. This practice promotes emotional intelligence and resilience.

Example Practice: When you feel a strong emotion, pause and identify the feeling. Ask yourself, "Where do I feel this in my body?" and breathe into that sensation.

Overcoming Common Obstacles to Mindfulness

It's common to face challenges when starting a mindfulness practice. Here are some common obstacles and tips to overcome them:

- **Mind Wandering**: It's natural for the mind to wander. Instead of feeling frustrated, gently guide your focus back to the present moment. Remember, noticing that your mind has wandered is a part of mindfulness practice.
- **Restlessness**: If sitting still feels uncomfortable, try a body scan meditation or a walking meditation. Movement can help anchor your focus.
- **Frustration**: It's important to recognize that mindfulness is a skill that takes time to develop. Embrace a growth mindset and celebrate small improvements.
- **Lack of Time**: Mindfulness doesn't have to take hours. Even dedicating one minute to mindful breathing or awareness can make a noticeable difference over time.

Incorporating Mindfulness into Daily Life

Mindfulness can be incorporated into any aspect of your life. Here are some tips for integrating mindfulness into your daily routine:

- **Mindful Breathing**: Take a few deep breaths throughout the day. Focus on the sensation of the air entering and leaving your body.
- **Mindful Eating**: Pay attention to the taste, texture, and smell of your food. Chew slowly and savor each bite.
- **Mindful Walking**: Focus on your footsteps and the sensations of walking, such as the feeling of your feet touching the ground.
- **Mindful Listening**: Listen attentively to others without interrupting. Notice the tone, emotion, and meaning behind their words.
- **Mindful Working**: Focus on one task at a time and avoid multitasking. Set clear intentions before starting your work.

The Science Behind Mindfulness

Research in neuroscience and psychology has demonstrated the profound effects of mindfulness on the brain and body. Mindfulness has been shown to reduce activity in the default mode network (DMN), the brain's "autopilot mode," which is linked to mind-wandering and rumination. This shift in brain activity enhances focus and fosters a sense of calm.

Additionally, mindfulness practice has been associated with increased gray matter density in brain regions involved in learning, memory, and emotional regulation. These changes underscore the potential of mindfulness to reshape the brain and improve overall well-being.

By practicing mindfulness regularly, you can transform your life, experiencing greater peace, joy, and fulfillment while equipping yourself with tools to navigate challenges with grace and resilience.

Chapter 03

Mindfulness Techniques for Beginners

Mindfulness Techniques: Practical Tools for a Mindful State

Mindfulness techniques are practical tools that can help you cultivate a more mindful state of being. These exercises are not just for relaxation; they actively train your mind to focus, observe, and live in the present moment. Here are some beginner-friendly techniques to get you started, along with insights into their benefits and practical tips to enhance your practice.

Mindfulness Breathing

Mindfulness breathing is one of the simplest and most effective ways to practice mindfulness. It anchors your attention to the present moment and calms the mind.

- **Find a quiet place**: Choose a peaceful environment where you won't be disturbed. If a quiet place is not available, use headphones with calming background music to create a personal bubble of tranquility.
- **Focus on your breath**: Pay attention to the sensation of your breath as it enters and leaves your body. Feel the air move through your nostrils and fill your lungs, and notice the natural rhythm of your breathing.
- **Count your breaths**: Count each inhale and exhale, starting from one and working your way up to ten. Counting helps to stabilize your attention and prevents your mind from wandering.
- **Return to the present**: If your mind wanders, gently bring it back to your breath. Wandering

thoughts are normal—acknowledge them without judgment and refocus on your breathing.

Benefits:

Mindful breathing activates the parasympathetic nervous system, reducing stress, lowering blood pressure, and improving mental clarity.

Body Scan Meditation

The body scan meditation is a powerful technique for cultivating awareness of bodily sensations and releasing tension.

- **Find a comfortable position**: Lie down or sit in a comfortable posture. Use cushions or a yoga mat to support your back.
- **Start at your toes**: Begin by focusing your attention on your toes, noticing any sensations such as tingling, warmth, or pressure.
- **Move slowly upwards**: Gradually shift your attention to your feet, calves, knees, thighs, and so on, until you reach the top of your head. Take your time with each area, allowing yourself to feel any tension or relaxation.
- **Return to the present**: If your mind wanders, gently bring it back to your body. Don't rush; let the process unfold naturally.

Benefits:

The body scan meditation improves your connection to your physical self, helping to alleviate chronic pain, reduce stress, and promote better sleep.

Practical Tip: For beginners, consider using guided body scan meditations available through apps or online platforms.

Walking Meditation

Walking meditation is a dynamic form of mindfulness that integrates movement with awareness.

- **Choose a peaceful location**: Find a quiet place to walk, such as a park or a nature trail. If outdoors is not feasible, practice indoors in a space with minimal distractions.
- **Focus on your steps**: Pay attention to the sensation of your feet touching the ground. Notice how your weight shifts with each step.
- **Notice your surroundings**: Observe the sights, sounds, and smells around you. Engage your senses fully and let them anchor you to the present moment.
- **Mindful breathing**: Continue to breathe deeply and mindfully as you walk. Synchronize your steps with your breaths for a deeper connection.

Benefits:

Walking meditation combines the calming effects of mindfulness with the health benefits of physical movement, making it an excellent practice for those who find sitting still challenging.

Practical Tip: Start with a slow pace and gradually integrate mindfulness into your regular walking routine.

Eating Meditation

Eating meditation transforms a routine activity into a mindful experience, enhancing your appreciation of food and improving digestion.

- **Choose a quiet place**: Find a peaceful place to eat your meal. A clutter-free, calm environment enhances the experience.
- **Focus on your food**: Pay attention to the appearance, smell, and taste of your food. Notice the colors, textures, and aromas.
- **Eat slowly and mindfully**: Take small bites and savor each mouthful. Chew thoroughly and relish the flavors.
- **Avoid distractions**: Turn off your phone and focus entirely on your meal. If eating with others, engage in mindful conversations without rushing through the meal.

Benefits:
Mindful eating helps you enjoy your meals more fully, prevents overeating, and promotes healthier eating habits.

Practical Tip: Start with a single piece of food, like a raisin or a slice of fruit, to practice eating meditation before applying it to full meals.

Mindfulness of Thoughts

Mindfulness of thoughts helps you become aware of your mental activity without being overwhelmed or controlled by it.

- **Observe your thoughts**: Notice your thoughts without judgment. Let them come and go, like clouds passing in the sky.
- **Let go of judgment**: Don't label your thoughts as good or bad. Accept them for what they are—mental events that do not define you.
- **Return to the present moment**: When your mind wanders, gently bring it back to the present moment. Use your breath or an external anchor, like a sound, to refocus.

Benefits:

Mindfulness of thoughts reduces overthinking, enhances emotional resilience, and improves decision-making by creating mental clarity.

Practical Tip: Keep a journal to record recurring thoughts and patterns. Writing them down can help you process them more effectively.

Overcoming Common Challenges in Mindfulness Practice

- **Impatience**: Many beginners expect immediate results, which can lead to frustration. Remember, mindfulness is a skill that develops over time. Treat it as a journey, not a destination.
- **Difficulty staying focused**: Use external anchors like sounds or sensations to guide your attention back to the present.
- **Lack of time**: Even five minutes of mindfulness practice can make a significant difference. Look

for small pockets of time during your day to practice.

- **Self-criticism**: Be kind to yourself. It's normal for the mind to wander — what matters is how you bring it back.

Enhancing Your Mindfulness Practice

To deepen your mindfulness practice:

- **Set intentions**: Start each session with a clear intention, such as reducing stress or cultivating gratitude.
- **Track progress**: Reflect on how mindfulness has impacted your mood, focus, and interactions.
- **Experiment with techniques**: Try different exercises to find what resonates best with you.

By practicing these techniques regularly, you can develop a stronger mindfulness practice and reap the benefits of a calmer, more focused mind. Remember, it's important to be patient with yourself and not to get discouraged if your mind wanders. The key is to keep returning to the present moment.

Chapter 04

Advanced Mindfulness Techniques

Advanced Mindfulness Practices

While the basic techniques of mindfulness are simple and accessible, advanced techniques can offer deeper levels of insight and transformation. These practices can help you cultivate compassion, expand your awareness, and achieve profound states of mental clarity and peace. Here are a few advanced mindfulness practices to explore in greater depth:

Loving-Kindness Meditation

Loving-kindness meditation (Metta Bhavana) involves cultivating feelings of love, compassion, and kindness towards oneself and others. This practice not only enhances emotional well-being but also fosters a sense of connection with others.

- **Start with self-compassion**: Begin by directing loving-kindness towards yourself. For example, silently repeat phrases like *"May I be happy, may I be healthy, may I live with ease."*
- **Expand your circle of compassion**: Gradually extend your feelings of love and kindness to others, such as friends, family, and acquaintances. Visualize their faces as you send them wishes for their well-being.
- **Universal love**: Ultimately, you can extend your love and compassion to all beings, including those you may find challenging to connect with.

Benefits:
Practicing loving-kindness meditation reduces feelings

of anger, resentment, and isolation while increasing empathy and social connectedness.

Practical Tip: If you're struggling to feel compassion for others, start by focusing on someone you deeply care for, and gradually include others.

Compassion Meditation

Compassion meditation focuses on cultivating feelings of compassion for the suffering of others. This practice fosters a deep understanding of shared human experiences and nurtures a desire to alleviate suffering.

- **Reflect on suffering**: Consider the suffering of others, both near and far. Reflect on their challenges, fears, or pain.
- **Cultivate empathy**: Try to understand the feelings of others by imagining yourself in their situation. This deepens your sense of connection.
- **Generate a wish to relieve suffering**: Silently wish for the happiness and well-being of others. For example, repeat phrases like *"May you be free from suffering, may you find peace."*

Benefits:
Compassion meditation enhances emotional resilience, reduces negative emotional responses, and fosters a sense of purpose by connecting you with the broader human condition.

Metta Meditation

Metta meditation is a specific form of loving-kindness practice, emphasizing goodwill towards oneself and others.

- **Start with self-love**: Begin by sending loving-kindness to yourself. Affirm positive intentions such as *"May I be safe, may I be content."*
- **Expand your circle of love**: Gradually extend these affirmations to loved ones, acquaintances, and even individuals you may feel neutral or negative towards.
- **Cultivate universal love**: Ultimately, extend your goodwill to all beings, transcending personal connections.

Benefits:
Metta meditation fosters forgiveness, reduces interpersonal conflict, and strengthens positive relationships.

Practical Tip: Practice this meditation during emotionally challenging times to shift your perspective from anger to understanding.

Vipassana Meditation

Vipassana meditation, meaning "insight" in Pali, focuses on observing the present moment without judgment. This practice cultivates self-awareness and a deep understanding of the impermanence of thoughts, emotions, and sensations.

- **Mindfulness of the body**: Pay attention to the sensations of your body, such as the rise and fall of your breath or the feeling of tension or relaxation in your muscles.
- **Mindfulness of feelings**: Observe your emotions without judgment. Acknowledge feelings of joy, anger, or sadness as they arise, and allow them to pass naturally.
- **Mindfulness of thoughts**: Notice your thoughts as they arise and fade. Avoid attaching to or analyzing them—simply observe.

Benefits:
Vipassana meditation enhances clarity of thought, reduces mental clutter, and helps practitioners achieve a sense of detachment from troubling emotions.

Practical Tip: Attend a Vipassana retreat for immersive training in this technique, which is traditionally taught in silence over several days.

Zen Meditation

Zen meditation (Zazen) is a discipline rooted in Zen Buddhism that emphasizes simplicity and direct experience. It involves sitting in a meditative posture and observing the mind and body.

- **The Zazen posture**: Sit in a comfortable, upright position, either on a cushion or a chair. Ensure your back is straight but not stiff. Rest your hands in your lap or on your knees.
- **Focus on the breath**: Pay attention to the sensation of your breath as it enters and leaves

your body. Count your breaths if it helps you maintain focus.

- **Mindful awareness**: Be aware of your thoughts, emotions, and sensations without judgment. Practice letting go of any distractions that arise.

Benefits:
Zen meditation fosters a sense of simplicity, calm, and insight, making it an ideal practice for achieving a state of "no-mind" (Mushin) where thoughts no longer dominate the mind.

Practical Tip: Incorporate Zen meditation into your daily routine, even for just 10–15 minutes, to develop consistency and deepen your practice.

Overcoming Challenges in Advanced Practices

Advanced mindfulness practices often bring up challenges as they delve deeper into your psyche. Here are some common obstacles and how to address them:

- **Difficulty sustaining focus**: Use guided meditations to help maintain focus during longer sessions.
- **Emotional intensity**: Advanced practices can surface deep emotions. Approach these moments with self-compassion and seek guidance if needed.
- **Impatience**: The benefits of advanced practices may take time to manifest. Trust the process and remain consistent.

Integrating Advanced Mindfulness into Daily Life

To make these practices a part of your life:

- **Set aside dedicated time**: Carve out specific times for advanced meditation practices to build consistency.
- **Combine practices**: Experiment by combining different techniques, such as starting with mindfulness breathing and transitioning into compassion meditation.
- **Reflect on your progress**: Maintain a journal to record your experiences, insights, and challenges. This can help you recognize your growth over time.

By practicing these advanced techniques, you can deepen your mindfulness practice and experience greater peace, clarity, and insight. Each of these methods is a pathway to discovering a richer and more meaningful connection with yourself and the world around you.

Chapter 05

Mindfulness for Stress Reduction

Managing Stress with Mindfulness

Stress is a common human experience that can negatively impact our mental and physical health. Mindfulness serves as a powerful tool for managing stress, promoting relaxation, and improving overall well-being. This chapter explores the connection between mindfulness and stress management, delving into practical techniques and their benefits.

The Science of Stress

Stress triggers the release of hormones like cortisol and adrenaline, activating the body's fight-or-flight response. While this response is essential in short bursts for survival, chronic stress can disrupt the body's equilibrium, leading to:

- **Mental health challenges**: Anxiety, depression, and difficulty concentrating.
- **Physical health issues**: Heart disease, digestive problems, and weakened immune function.
- **Behavioral changes**: Irritability, overeating, or disrupted sleep patterns.

How mindfulness helps: Mindfulness engages the parasympathetic nervous system, encouraging relaxation and countering the effects of chronic stress. It helps regulate cortisol levels, allowing the body to recover and restore balance.

Mindfulness Techniques for Stress Relief

Here are some effective mindfulness practices for stress relief, along with additional insights on how to incorporate them into your daily routine:

Mindful Breathing:
Focus on your breath as it enters and leaves your body. For example:

1. Inhale for a count of four, hold for a count of four, and exhale for a count of six.
2. Visualize stress leaving your body with every exhale.

Benefit: Mindful breathing calms the nervous system, reduces heart rate, and brings immediate relief during stressful moments.

Body Scan Meditation:
Gradually focus on each part of your body, starting from your toes and moving upward. Release any tension you feel along the way.

Pair this practice with progressive muscle relaxation for deeper stress relief.

Benefit: This technique enhances body awareness and helps release physical tension caused by stress.

Mindful Walking:
Pay attention to the sensations of walking, the

sounds around you, and the feeling of the ground beneath your feet.

- Practice this in nature to amplify the calming effects.

  Benefit: Combining mindfulness with physical activity helps clear the mind and reduce stress hormones.

Mindful Eating:
Eat slowly, focusing on the taste, texture, and smell of your food.

- Before eating, take a moment to express gratitude for the meal.

  Benefit: Mindful eating not only reduces stress but also promotes healthier eating habits and improved digestion.

Yoga and Tai Chi:
These practices combine physical movement with mindfulness.

- Choose beginner-friendly routines focusing on gentle stretches and deep breathing.

  Benefit: Yoga and Tai Chi improve flexibility, balance, and emotional regulation, making them ideal for stress management.

Mindfulness and Anxiety

Anxiety often involves racing thoughts and fears about the future. Mindfulness teaches you to observe these thoughts and feelings without judgment.

- **Observing without attachment**: Recognize anxious thoughts as transient and separate from your true self.
- **Grounding exercises**: Use the "5-4-3-2-1" technique, identifying five things you see, four you can touch, three you hear, two you smell, and one you taste.

How it helps: By bringing attention to the present moment, mindfulness reduces the intensity of anxious feelings and prevents spirals into overwhelming worry.

Mindfulness and Depression

Depression often involves negative thought patterns and feelings of hopelessness. Mindfulness can interrupt these patterns by increasing awareness and encouraging a more balanced perspective.

- **Challenging negative thoughts**: Use mindfulness to identify and question unhelpful beliefs. For example, ask yourself: *Is this thought a fact, or just an interpretation?*
- **Gratitude practice**: Pair mindfulness with gratitude journaling to shift focus toward positive aspects of life.

How it helps: Regular mindfulness practice strengthens the prefrontal cortex, enhancing emotional regulation and reducing depressive symptoms.

Mindfulness and Burnout

Burnout results from prolonged stress and manifests as emotional, physical, and mental exhaustion. Mindfulness can prevent and alleviate burnout by fostering resilience and emotional balance.

- **Micro-mindfulness breaks**: Take short mindfulness pauses throughout the day. For example, spend two minutes focusing on your breath or observing your surroundings.
- **Mindful work habits**: Use mindfulness to manage workloads by breaking tasks into smaller, manageable steps.

How it helps: Mindfulness restores energy levels, sharpens focus, and encourages a healthier work-life balance, reducing the risk of burnout.

Incorporating Mindfulness into Daily Life

Consistency is key to reaping the benefits of mindfulness for stress management.

- **Start small**: Begin with 5-10 minutes a day and gradually increase the duration of your practice.
- **Use reminders**: Set alerts on your phone or place sticky notes in visible areas to prompt mindfulness breaks.

- **Combine with daily activities**: Practice mindfulness while brushing your teeth, washing dishes, or commuting.

The Long-Term Benefits of Mindfulness for Stress Relief

Studies show that regular mindfulness practice can lead to:

- Lower cortisol levels and reduced blood pressure.
- Enhanced emotional resilience and improved mood.
- Better sleep quality and overall physical health.

Remember, it takes time and patience to develop a regular mindfulness practice. Treat it as a journey, not a destination, and celebrate small victories along the way.

Chapter 06

Mindfulness for Improved Focus and Concentration

Enhancing Focus and Productivity with Mindfulness

In today's fast-paced world, maintaining focus and productivity can feel like an uphill battle. Mindfulness offers practical techniques to train your brain, improve concentration, and unlock your full potential. This chapter explores the science of attention, mindfulness strategies for focus, and tips to overcome distractions.

The Science of Attention

Attention is a finite resource. Neuroscience shows that our brains are designed to focus on one task at a time, and multitasking often leads to decreased efficiency and higher stress levels. Here's a deeper look at how attention works:

- **The role of the prefrontal cortex**: This brain region controls attention and decision-making. Mindfulness strengthens the prefrontal cortex, enhancing focus and reducing impulsivity.
- **Switching costs**: Every time you shift your focus between tasks, your brain uses additional energy and time to reorient itself, reducing overall productivity.

How mindfulness helps: Regular mindfulness practice trains the brain to stay present, minimizing the urge to multitask and improving sustained attention over time.

Mindfulness Techniques for Better Focus

Incorporate these mindfulness strategies into your daily life to sharpen focus and concentration:

Mindful Breathing:

Practice deep, intentional breathing:

1. Inhale for four seconds, hold for four seconds, and exhale for six seconds.
2. As you breathe, silently count each inhale and exhale to anchor your attention.

Benefit: This technique calms the mind and improves your ability to concentrate during challenging tasks.

Mindful Meditation:

Dedicate at least 10 minutes a day to meditation. Focus on your breath, a mantra, or a visualization.

- Apps like Headspace or Calm can guide beginners through meditation practices.

Benefit: Over time, meditation improves working memory and reduces mind-wandering.

Mindful Working:

Use the Pomodoro technique:

1. Work in 25-minute intervals, focusing on one task.
2. Take a 5-minute mindful break between intervals.

Benefit: This approach prevents burnout and enhances deep work sessions.

Mindful Breaks:
Integrate short, restorative pauses into your day:

- Use breaks to stretch, practice deep breathing, or observe your surroundings without judgment.

Benefit: These breaks reduce mental fatigue and restore energy for sustained productivity.

Mindful Listening:
Practice active listening by giving your full attention to the speaker:

- Avoid interrupting or multitasking during conversations.
- Reflect on what you've heard before responding.

Benefit: Mindful listening improves communication skills and strengthens relationships.

Mindfulness and Productivity

Mindfulness directly impacts productivity by:

- **Reducing stress**: A calmer mind works more efficiently.
- **Boosting creativity**: Mindfulness enhances divergent thinking, allowing for innovative problem-solving.

- **Improving decision-making**: By fostering clarity and focus, mindfulness helps you make thoughtful choices.

Overcoming Distractions

In a world filled with digital distractions, staying focused requires deliberate effort. Mindfulness equips you with the tools to manage interruptions effectively.

Set boundaries:
Designate phone-free times or create a schedule for checking social media and emails.

- **Use settings like** "Do Not Disturb" during focus sessions.

Benefit: Limiting access to distractions helps maintain concentration on high-priority tasks.

Create a distraction-free workspace:
Optimize your environment for focus:

- Keep your workspace clean and organized.
- Use noise-canceling headphones if necessary.

Benefit: A well-organized space reduces cognitive overload and encourages productivity.

Leverage productivity tools:
Explore apps like Freedom, Focus@Will, or Forest to block distractions and track time spent on tasks.

Benefit: These tools provide structure and accountability for staying on track.

Practice mindfulness meditation:
Regular meditation trains your brain to resist the pull of distractions, fostering better self-discipline over time.

The Long-Term Benefits of Mindfulness for Focus and Productivity

Developing a mindfulness practice requires patience and consistency. Over time, the benefits become more apparent:

- **Improved sustained attention**: Mindfulness increases your capacity to focus on tasks for extended periods without fatigue.
- **Enhanced resilience**: A mindful approach to setbacks reduces stress and promotes faster recovery.
- **Greater life satisfaction**: Mindfulness encourages a balanced perspective, helping you prioritize what truly matters.

By incorporating mindfulness into your daily routine, you can overcome distractions, maximize your productivity, and enjoy a more focused, fulfilling life. Remember, the key to success lies in persistence and self-compassion. Treat every moment of practice as a step toward becoming the best version of yourself.

Chapter 07

Mindfulness for Emotional Intelligence

Emotional Intelligence and Mindfulness: Building Stronger Connections

Emotional intelligence—the ability to understand, regulate, and effectively express emotions—plays a pivotal role in achieving personal and professional success. Mindfulness can serve as a powerful tool to enhance emotional intelligence by cultivating self-awareness, emotional regulation, empathy, and communication skills. This chapter explores how mindfulness contributes to emotional growth and practical strategies to integrate it into your life.

Understanding Emotions

Emotions are multifaceted and can often feel overwhelming. Mindfulness allows us to observe emotions as they arise, fostering a deeper understanding of their origins and significance.

- **The Role of Triggers**: Emotions often stem from specific triggers, such as situations, people, or past experiences. Mindfulness helps us recognize these triggers and develop healthier responses.
- **Positive vs. Negative Emotions**: While positive emotions, such as joy and gratitude, uplift us, negative emotions like anger or sadness can offer insights when approached mindfully.
- **Emotional Patterns**: Over time, mindfulness can reveal recurring emotional patterns, enabling us to break free from unproductive cycles.

Enhancement Tip: Journaling your emotions mindfully at the end of the day can provide clarity about patterns and triggers.

Emotional Regulation Techniques

Mindfulness equips us with tools to manage emotions effectively. Expanding on these techniques:

Mindful Breathing:

- Use the "4-7-8" breathing technique: Inhale for 4 seconds, hold for 7 seconds, and exhale for 8 seconds.
- This method calms the nervous system, particularly during heightened emotional states.

Body Scan Meditation:

- Incorporate progressive relaxation into your body scans, consciously releasing tension in each muscle group.
- Pair this with affirmations, such as "I am grounded" or "I am calm."

Emotional Labeling:

- Use a broader vocabulary to describe emotions. For example, instead of "angry," specify "frustrated," "irritated," or "resentful."
- Reflect on what may have caused the specific emotion, enhancing understanding and control.

Building Emotional Resilience

Emotional resilience helps us recover from setbacks and navigate life's challenges with grace. Mindfulness strengthens resilience through intentional practices:

Cultivating Gratitude:

- Start a gratitude journal. Each day, list three things you're grateful for, no matter how small.
- Reflect on these entries during tough times to maintain a balanced perspective.

Self-Compassion Practices:

- Use self-compassion phrases like, "May I be kind to myself," or, "It's okay to feel this way."
- Imagine how you would comfort a close friend and apply that same kindness to yourself.

Strengthening Support Systems:

- Engage in mindful interactions with loved ones by setting aside uninterrupted time to connect.
- Regularly express appreciation to deepen your bonds and enhance mutual support.

Practicing Empathy

Empathy bridges the gap between individuals, fostering stronger, more meaningful relationships. Mindfulness nurtures empathy by sharpening our ability to be present with others.

Active Listening:

- Avoid formulating responses while the other person is speaking.
- Practice reflective listening by summarizing what the other person has shared.

Perspective-Taking:

- Use mindfulness to imagine the other person's feelings and challenges without judgment.
- Ask questions like, "What might they be experiencing right now?"

Compassionate Communication:

- Begin conversations with phrases like, "I understand how you feel," or, "I can see why this matters to you."
- Avoid defensive language, focusing instead on creating a collaborative dialogue.

Improving Communication Skills

Mindfulness transforms communication, making it more intentional and impactful. Here's how you can refine your interactions:

Mindful Speaking:

- Pause briefly before speaking to ensure your words align with your intentions.
- When addressing conflicts, use "I" statements, such as "I feel hurt when..." instead of accusatory language.

Non-Verbal Communication:

- Observe your posture, facial expressions, and gestures. Mindfulness increases awareness of how these non-verbal cues influence your message.
- Mirror the other person's tone or body language subtly to build rapport.

Reducing Miscommunication:

- During tense discussions, take mindful pauses to clarify misunderstandings before they escalate.
- Practice summarizing key points to ensure both parties are aligned.

Expanding Emotional Intelligence in Everyday Life

Mindfulness is not a quick fix; it is a practice that evolves over time. By consistently applying these techniques, you can experience long-term growth in emotional intelligence. Benefits include:

- **Stronger Interpersonal Relationships**: Improved empathy and communication foster deeper connections.

  - **Reduced Emotional Reactivity**: Mindfulness helps you respond thoughtfully rather than react impulsively.
  - **Greater Self-Confidence**: Understanding and managing your emotions boosts self-assurance in challenging situations.

Through mindfulness, you can unlock the full potential of your emotional intelligence, enriching your life with deeper self-awareness, emotional balance, and meaningful relationships. The journey may require effort and patience, but the rewards are transformative.

Chapter 08

Mindfulness for Creativity and Innovation

Mindfulness and Creativity: Unlocking Your Full Potential

Creativity and innovation are indispensable for solving problems, identifying opportunities, and generating new ideas. Mindfulness serves as a catalyst for these skills by fostering focus, reducing stress, and nurturing an open and curious mind. This chapter explores how mindfulness can enhance creativity and innovation while offering strategies for overcoming creative blocks and cultivating a creative mindset.

The Mindful Creative Process

The creative process is a synergy of conscious and unconscious thought, where mindfulness plays a pivotal role in nurturing ideas and executing them effectively. Let's delve deeper into each step of the mindful creative process:

Mindful Preparation:

- **Creating an Inspiring Space**: Design a workspace that minimizes distractions. Include elements that stimulate creativity, such as artwork, plants, or natural lighting.
- **Mental Preparation**: Before starting, take a few minutes to engage in mindful breathing or visualization. Picture yourself successfully navigating the creative task.

Mindful Generation:

- **Enhanced Brainstorming**: Set a timer and jot down as many ideas as possible without judgment. This time-constrained exercise encourages spontaneity.
- **Mind Mapping**: Use a central concept and branch out to explore related ideas visually, enhancing connections.
- **Free Writing**: Write continuously for a set period without worrying about grammar or coherence to unlock subconscious ideas.

Mindful Evaluation:

- Adopt a "beginner's mind" when reviewing ideas. Assess them objectively, as if encountering them for the first time.
- Categorize ideas into actionable, exploratory, or experimental, ensuring a balanced approach to execution.

Mindful Execution:

- Break tasks into smaller, manageable steps to maintain focus. Use techniques like the Pomodoro Technique to work in focused intervals.
- Acknowledge distractions but gently redirect your attention to the task at hand.

Mindful Reflection:

- After completing the process, reflect on what worked well and what could improve. Use questions like: "What inspired me most?" or "Where did I feel resistance?"

- Keep a creativity journal to document your process, thoughts, and breakthroughs for future reference.

Overcoming Creative Blocks

Creative blocks can be daunting, but mindfulness offers tools to overcome them. Expanding on strategies:

Take a Break:

Engage in activities that rejuvenate your mind, such as walking in nature or listening to music. Studies show that stepping away allows the subconscious to process ideas.

Mindfulness Meditation:

Try a guided visualization focusing on creativity. Imagine a flowing river, with ideas floating freely, accessible to your mind.

Engage in Creative Activities:

Explore hobbies unrelated to your primary creative goal. For example, painting or playing an instrument can reignite inspiration.

Collaborate with Others:

Use group brainstorming techniques like "yes, and..." where participants build on each other's ideas, fostering a positive and collaborative environment.

Embrace Failure:

Reframe failure as a learning opportunity. For example, Thomas Edison viewed every unsuccessful experiment as a step closer to discovering the light bulb.

Pro Tip: Keep a "failure journal" to record lessons learned from setbacks and reflect on your growth over time.

Cultivating a Creative Mindset

A creative mindset thrives on curiosity, openness, and resilience. Mindfulness cultivates these qualities, enabling you to think outside the box and embrace challenges.

Ask Questions:

Start with "why," "what if," and "how" to spark curiosity. For instance, ask, "What if I approached this problem from a completely different angle?"

Challenge Assumptions:

Regularly question the status quo. Use techniques like reverse thinking (e.g., "What would happen if I did the opposite of what's expected?").

Embrace Failure:

Develop a ritual to celebrate small failures. This practice can reduce fear and make experimentation feel rewarding.

Take Risks:

Experiment with low-stakes projects to build confidence in taking creative risks. For example, try writing a short story in a genre you're unfamiliar with.

Practice Gratitude:

Daily gratitude practices can enhance your perception of possibilities and abundance, fueling creativity. For example, write about moments that brought joy or inspiration.

Mindfulness and Innovation in Practice

Applying mindfulness in professional or personal innovation can lead to groundbreaking results. Here are some practical examples:

- **Creative Problem-Solving**: Mindfulness helps uncover innovative solutions by allowing you to approach problems with fresh perspectives. Use meditation to focus solely on the problem and allow intuitive insights to arise.
- **Team Innovation**: In collaborative settings, practicing mindful listening ensures that every idea is heard and valued, fostering a more inclusive and innovative environment.
- **Sustaining Innovation**: Build a routine that incorporates mindfulness into daily creative tasks, ensuring long-term growth and consistency in innovation.

Unlocking Your Creative Potential

Mindfulness is the key to unlocking your creative potential. It invites you to approach creativity with a calm, focused, and curious mind, free from the constraints of stress and self-doubt. By integrating mindfulness into your daily routines and creative practices, you can not only generate innovative ideas but also execute them with clarity and purpose

Chapter 09

Mindfulness for Better Sleep

Understanding the Importance of Sleep for Mental Health

Sleep is not just a physical requirement; it plays a crucial role in maintaining mental health. Poor sleep quality can lead to heightened stress, anxiety, and depression. When you incorporate mindfulness techniques, your mind and body align, promoting deeper and more restorative sleep.

Mindfulness helps regulate cortisol levels (stress hormones) and promotes the production of melatonin, the hormone responsible for sleep. By addressing the root causes of insomnia, such as racing thoughts and chronic stress, mindfulness allows your brain to relax and prepare for restful sleep.

The Science of Sleep and Its Connection to Productivity

Good sleep directly influences cognitive functions like focus, memory, and problem-solving abilities. Research shows that REM sleep is essential for creative thinking and emotional processing, while deep non-REM sleep aids in physical restoration and immune system support.

Practicing mindfulness before bedtime helps transition the brain from a high-alert state to a relaxed mode, preparing you for optimal sleep cycles. The quality of these cycles determines how refreshed and productive you feel the next day.

Expanding on Mindfulness Techniques for Better Sleep

Progressive Muscle Relaxation:
Start by tensing and releasing each muscle group, starting from your toes and moving upward. This technique helps relieve built-up tension in the body and prepares you for a peaceful sleep.

Visualization Techniques:
Visualize calming scenarios, such as walking along a beach or sitting by a serene lake. Engaging your imagination in this way can slow down mental chatter and help you relax.

Mindful Journaling:
Before bedtime, write down any racing thoughts, worries, or plans for the next day. By emptying your mind onto paper, you create space for rest and clarity.

Using Mindfulness to Overcome Chronic Insomnia

Chronic insomnia often stems from an overactive mind, heightened stress, or irregular sleep schedules. Mindfulness targets these issues holistically:

- **Recognizing Thought Patterns:**
  Practice observing intrusive thoughts about not being able to sleep. This awareness helps you detach from these fears and minimizes their impact on your ability to fall asleep.

- **Gratitude Practice Before Sleep:**
Reflect on three things you're grateful for before bed. Gratitude shifts your focus from stress to positive emotions, creating a calming effect.

Creating a Sleep-Conducive Environment Through Mindfulness

Mindfulness goes beyond mental practices; it extends to the physical space where you sleep:

- **Declutter Your Bedroom:** A tidy space creates a calming atmosphere. Remove unnecessary distractions that might trigger stress.
- **Aromatherapy:** Use calming scents like lavender or chamomile to relax your senses and signal to your brain that it's time to sleep.
- **Adjusting Temperature:** Your bedroom temperature should ideally range between 60-67°F for optimal sleep. Being mindful of your comfort improves sleep quality.

Mindfulness-Based Cognitive Behavioral Therapy for Insomnia (CBT-I)

CBT-I is a structured approach combining mindfulness with cognitive-behavioral techniques. It addresses negative thought patterns around sleep, replacing them with positive associations. Mindfulness enhances CBT-I by grounding the mind, reducing the time it takes to fall asleep, and minimizing wakefulness during the night.

Tips for Mindful Waking to Improve Sleep Continuity

How you wake up sets the tone for your day and impacts your subsequent night's sleep:

- **Practice Gratitude:** Upon waking, take a moment to express gratitude for restful sleep.
- **Mindful Stretching:** Perform gentle stretches to awaken your muscles and signal your body to start the day.
- **Morning Meditation:** Begin your day with 5–10 minutes of mindfulness meditation. This practice establishes calmness and helps regulate your circadian rhythm.

Managing Sleep Disruptions with Mindfulness

Even with a strong routine, occasional disruptions can occur. Mindfulness offers tools to navigate them effectively:

- **Nighttime Anxiety Management:** If you wake up anxious, perform deep breathing exercises or repeat a calming mantra, such as "I am safe, and my mind is calm."
- **Short Mindfulness Practices:** A quick body scan or visualization exercise can help you transition back to sleep without frustration.

Chapter 10

Mindfulness for Physical Health

Deepening the Understanding of the Mind-Body Connection

The connection between the mind and body is bidirectional, meaning that physical health can influence mental well-being and vice versa. For example, when you're stressed, your body releases cortisol, a hormone that can suppress your immune system and increase inflammation. Over time, chronic stress can contribute to conditions like hypertension, diabetes, and even autoimmune disorders.

Conversely, when you practice mindfulness, you activate the parasympathetic nervous system (the "rest and digest" system), which reduces cortisol levels and promotes healing. Regular mindfulness practices help regulate heart rate, blood pressure, and digestion, enhancing your overall physical health.

Mindfulness for Managing Chronic Pain

Chronic pain can be debilitating, but mindfulness can provide relief by helping individuals shift their relationship with pain. Here's how:

- **Changing the Perception of Pain:** Pain often triggers negative emotions, which amplify suffering. Mindfulness encourages acceptance of the pain without attaching fear or frustration to it. This can reduce the perceived intensity of pain.
- **Engaging the Relaxation Response:** Mindfulness activates the relaxation response, reducing muscle tension and calming the nervous

system. This helps manage conditions like migraines, arthritis, and fibromyalgia.

- **Focused Breathing for Pain Relief:** Deep, mindful breathing can reduce the physiological stress response associated with pain, leading to improved comfort levels.

Mindful Eating for Sustainable Weight Management

Mindful eating not only helps manage weight but also improves digestion and reduces emotional eating. Here's how you can integrate mindful eating into your routine:

- **Awareness of Hunger and Satiety:** Before eating, pause and ask yourself if you're truly hungry or eating out of boredom, stress, or habit. During meals, focus on the sensations of fullness to avoid overeating.
- **Slowing Down Mealtime:** Chew slowly and savor each bite. This helps your brain catch up with your stomach, making you more aware of when you're full.
- **Recognizing Emotional Triggers:** Mindfulness helps identify emotions like stress or sadness that often lead to overeating. Addressing these emotions with mindfulness practices, like journaling or meditation, can prevent unhealthy eating patterns.

Mindful Exercise for Enhanced Physical Performance

Incorporating mindfulness into exercise not only improves physical fitness but also strengthens the mind-body connection:

- **Enhancing Focus:** Mindfulness allows you to focus on each movement, ensuring proper form and reducing the risk of injury. For example, during yoga or weightlifting, being fully present helps align your body and movements.
- **Connecting with Your Body:** Pay attention to how your muscles feel during different exercises. This awareness can help improve flexibility, coordination, and balance.
- **Using Breath to Enhance Performance:** Deep, mindful breathing during exercise can boost oxygen delivery to your muscles, improving endurance and reducing fatigue.

Mindful Eating and Long-Term Health Benefits

Mindful eating has far-reaching benefits beyond weight management:

- **Improving Digestion:** Eating slowly and chewing thoroughly can enhance digestion and nutrient absorption, reducing bloating and other gastrointestinal issues.
- **Reducing Inflammation:** Mindful food choices—such as selecting fresh, whole foods over processed items—can lower inflammation and the

risk of chronic diseases like diabetes and cardiovascular disorders.

- **Cultivating Gratitude for Food:** Taking a moment to appreciate where your food comes from can foster a deeper connection with your meals, encouraging healthier choices.

Using Mindfulness to Build Healthy Eating Habits

Mindfulness can help break unhealthy eating habits:

- **Identifying Triggers for Unhealthy Eating:** Notice patterns, such as eating sugary snacks during stress, and replace them with healthier options.
- **Practicing Portion Control:** Mindfulness encourages awareness of serving sizes, helping prevent overeating without the need for strict dieting.
- **Reducing Cravings:** Mindfulness-based strategies, such as focusing on your breath when a craving arises, can help you ride out the urge to eat unhealthy foods.

Practical Tips for Integrating Mindfulness Into Daily Life

To see long-term physical health benefits, incorporate these mindful practices into your routine:

- **Morning Stretching:** Begin your day with mindful stretching to awaken your body and improve flexibility.

- **Mindful Hydration:** Pay attention to how your body feels as you drink water throughout the day. This can help you stay adequately hydrated.
- **Mindful Walking:** During walks, notice the rhythm of your steps and the feel of the ground beneath your feet. This practice is particularly effective for reducing stress and enhancing cardiovascular health.

Mindfulness for Strengthening the Immune System

Mindfulness can improve immune function through stress reduction:

- **Reducing Inflammation:** Chronic stress triggers inflammation, weakening the immune system. Mindfulness reduces stress, helping your body fight infections more effectively.
- **Balancing Hormones:** Regular mindfulness practices promote hormonal balance, boosting immunity and energy levels.

Tracking Progress in Mindfulness and Physical Health

To gauge the impact of mindfulness on your physical health, consider keeping a journal:

- Track improvements in energy levels, sleep quality, and digestion.
- Note reductions in physical symptoms, such as pain or stress-induced headaches.

- Reflect on how mindfulness has influenced your eating and exercise habits.

Chapter 11

Mindfulness for Relationships

Deepening the Practice of Mindful Communication

Mindful communication is not just about speaking and listening but also about cultivating an awareness of how our words and actions impact others. Here's how you can enhance mindful communication:

- **Active Listening Beyond Words:** Pay attention not only to the speaker's words but also to their emotions and body language. Often, what someone doesn't say is just as important as what they do.
- **Creating Safe Spaces for Dialogue:** Mindfulness helps us create environments where others feel safe expressing themselves without fear of judgment or criticism. Pause before responding and ask open-ended questions to show genuine interest.
- **Mindful Pauses During Conversations:** When emotions run high, take a moment to breathe deeply before responding. This helps prevent reactive communication and promotes thoughtful dialogue.

Strengthening Empathy Through Mindfulness

Empathy is the cornerstone of healthy relationships, and mindfulness can deepen our ability to understand and share the feelings of others:

- **Developing Emotional Awareness:** Mindfulness helps you become more aware of your emotions, making it easier to recognize and empathize with others' emotions. For example, you can notice when a loved one is upset even if they don't say it outright.

- **Imagining Perspectives:** Practice putting yourself in the other person's shoes. Imagine how you would feel in their situation and how you would like to be treated.
- **Non-verbal Empathy:** Show empathy not just through words but also through kind gestures, such as a reassuring touch or a warm smile.

Resolving Conflict Mindfully: Going Deeper

Conflicts are opportunities for growth if approached mindfully. Here's how mindfulness can enhance conflict resolution:

- **Managing Emotional Triggers:** Conflicts often arise because of emotional reactions. Mindfulness helps you identify your triggers, such as feeling dismissed or misunderstood, so you can respond calmly instead of reacting impulsively.
- **Setting Boundaries Mindfully:** During conflicts, it's important to express your limits respectfully. Use "I" statements, such as "I feel upset when..." instead of blaming the other person.
- **Acknowledging Shared Goals:** Mindfulness allows you to focus on what both parties want to achieve. This shifts the focus from "winning" the argument to finding a mutually beneficial solution.
- **Breathing to Stay Calm:** If emotions escalate during a conflict, take a few deep breaths to regain

composure and clarity before continuing the conversation.

Practicing Forgiveness Through Mindfulness

Forgiveness is a mindful act that benefits both the forgiver and the forgiven. It's not about condoning harmful behavior but about releasing the burden of resentment:

- **Releasing the Past:** Mindfulness encourages living in the present. Holding onto past grievances keeps you stuck in negative emotions. Forgiveness allows you to move forward.
- **Self-Compassion in Forgiveness:** Sometimes, the hardest person to forgive is yourself. Mindfulness teaches self-compassion, helping you let go of guilt and regret.
- **Rituals for Forgiveness:** Consider writing a letter (even if you don't send it) or meditating on feelings of compassion to help release anger and resentment.

Building Emotional Intimacy Through Mindfulness

Mindfulness can help strengthen the emotional bonds in your relationships:

- **Cultivating Vulnerability:** Mindfulness allows you to open up about your thoughts and feelings without fear of judgment, fostering deeper emotional intimacy.

- **Mindful Appreciation of Others:** Spend a few moments each day reflecting on the positive qualities of your loved ones. Share these observations with them to deepen your connection.
- **Engaging in Shared Mindfulness Practices:** Activities like meditating or practicing yoga together can create shared moments of mindfulness and strengthen your bond.

Mindful Acts of Kindness

Kindness strengthens relationships and spreads positivity. Mindful acts of kindness go beyond grand gestures and focus on genuine care:

- **Being Present in Kindness:** When performing an act of kindness, give your full attention to the other person. For instance, when helping a loved one, listen to their needs and respond with compassion.
- **Spontaneous Kindness:** Look for opportunities in everyday life, such as helping someone carry groceries, leaving a thoughtful note, or offering words of encouragement.

Spending Quality Time Mindfully

Mindful quality time means being fully present with loved ones:

- **Device-Free Interactions:** Put away distractions like phones during family meals or conversations to foster meaningful connections.

- **Engaging in Shared Hobbies:** Doing activities you both enjoy, like cooking, hiking, or playing games, can create lasting memories.
- **Active Gratitude:** Express appreciation for the time you spend together. Even a simple "I enjoy spending time with you" can strengthen bonds.

Mindfulness in Everyday Interactions

Mindfulness isn't limited to major conflicts or deep conversations. It can transform everyday interactions:

- **Greeting with Intention:** Start your day by warmly greeting loved ones, setting a positive tone for your interactions.
- **Practicing Patience:** Whether waiting in line with a partner or listening to a child's story, mindfulness helps you stay present and patient.
- **Being Attuned to Non-verbal Cues:** Notice subtle signs, like a friend's slumped shoulders, that may indicate they need support.

Chapter 12

Mindfulness for Children

Understanding the Importance of Early Mindfulness Practices

Children are in a formative stage where habits, emotional responses, and mental patterns are being shaped. Introducing mindfulness early can set the foundation for a lifetime of resilience and emotional well-being:

- **Why Start Young?**: At a young age, children's brains are highly adaptable. Mindfulness helps them develop emotional regulation, focus, and empathy, which are critical life skills.
- **Lifelong Benefits**: When mindfulness becomes a habit early in life, it is more likely to carry into adulthood, fostering healthier stress responses and better relationships.
- **Neuroplasticity in Children**: Research shows that mindfulness practices can positively influence brain development in children, particularly in areas related to focus and emotional regulation.

Age-Appropriate Techniques for Mindfulness

Different age groups respond better to mindfulness techniques tailored to their developmental stage:

- **Preschoolers**: Use playful activities like pretending to blow up a balloon while practicing deep breathing or focusing on a favorite stuffed animal during meditation.
- **Elementary-Aged Children**: Incorporate storytelling with mindfulness themes or create simple gratitude journals.

- **Teens**: Teach reflective journaling, gratitude practices, and mindful movement, such as yoga, to align with their growing need for independence and self-expression.

Integrating Mindfulness into Everyday Life

Mindfulness can be seamlessly woven into daily routines:

- **Morning Rituals**: Start the day with a quick breathing exercise to help your child prepare for school or activities.
- **Bedtime Mindfulness**: Use body scan meditations to help your child relax and fall asleep more easily.
- **Mindful Transitions**: Practice mindfulness during transitions, like moving from playtime to homework, to make the shift smoother and less stressful.

Making Mindfulness Fun and Engaging

Children are more likely to engage with mindfulness practices that are enjoyable and creative:

- **Mindfulness Games**: Introduce simple games like "The Stillness Challenge," where children see who can remain quiet and still the longest.
- **Mindful Art**: Encourage your child to draw or paint their emotions as a way of exploring and expressing feelings.
- **Mindful Nature Walks**: Take your child outdoors and encourage them to notice the sounds, smells, and sights of nature.

Addressing Resistance to Mindfulness

Some children may initially resist mindfulness practices, especially if they find it challenging to stay still or focused. Here's how to address this resistance:

- **Start Small**: Begin with short, two-minute exercises and gradually increase the duration as your child becomes more comfortable.
- **Be Patient**: Understand that mindfulness is a skill that takes time to develop. Avoid forcing the practice; instead, make it a natural part of daily life.
- **Celebrate Small Wins**: Praise your child for participating, even if they only manage a short session. Positive reinforcement encourages consistency.

Supporting Emotional Development with Mindfulness

Mindfulness can help children navigate complex emotions as they grow:

- **Emotional Awareness**: Teach children to identify their feelings without judgment. For example, they can use phrases like, "I feel angry right now, and that's okay."
- **Labeling Emotions**: Encourage your child to put words to their emotions, which helps them understand and regulate their feelings.
- **Mindfulness During Emotional Outbursts**: Teach your child to pause and take three deep

breaths during moments of anger or frustration to regain control.

Helping Children Cope with Stress and Anxiety

Mindfulness is a powerful tool for addressing childhood stress and anxiety:

- **Calm Down Jars**: Create a jar filled with glitter and water. Shake it and encourage your child to watch the glitter settle, using the time to breathe deeply.
- **Anchoring Techniques**: Teach children to focus on a physical sensation, like feeling their feet on the ground, when they feel overwhelmed.
- **Storytelling for Relaxation**: Use guided imagery through storytelling, like asking them to imagine being a tree with deep, calming roots.

Mindful Parent-Child Bonding Activities

Incorporating mindfulness into shared activities strengthens the parent-child bond:

- **Joint Gratitude Practices**: Spend a few minutes before bed sharing things you're grateful for. This fosters positivity and connection.
- **Shared Breathing Exercises**: Practice deep breathing together to create a sense of calm and unity.
- **Mindful Cooking**: Involve your child in preparing a meal mindfully, focusing on the smells, textures, and flavors of the ingredients.

Mindfulness and Academic Success

Mindfulness is linked to better focus, memory, and emotional regulation, which can improve academic performance:

- **Improved Concentration**: Mindfulness trains children to focus on one task at a time, reducing distractions during homework or lessons.
- **Managing Test Anxiety**: Teach mindful breathing exercises before exams to help children stay calm and focused.
- **Creating Study Rituals**: Encourage mindful study sessions where children set intentions and take mindful breaks to avoid burnout.

Mindfulness as a Lifelong Skill

When children learn mindfulness, they carry these skills into adulthood:

- **Building Resilience**: Mindfulness helps children develop coping strategies for challenges they may face later in life.
- **Fostering Empathy and Kindness**: Children who practice mindfulness are more likely to grow into compassionate adults.
- **Encouraging Self-Care**: Mindfulness teaches the importance of taking time for mental and emotional well-being, a skill they can rely on throughout their lives.

Chapter 13

Mindfulness in the Workplace

How Can Mindfulness Address Workplace Challenges?

Mindfulness can serve as an effective tool to address common workplace challenges such as high stress levels, communication breakdowns, and declining morale:

- **Reducing Burnout**: Mindfulness helps employees recognize early signs of burnout and encourages regular breaks to recharge mentally and physically.
- **Improving Interpersonal Relationships**: Mindfulness promotes empathy and understanding, which can reduce conflicts and foster a more collaborative environment.
- **Enhancing Emotional Regulation**: Employees who practice mindfulness are better equipped to manage frustration, anger, or anxiety during high-pressure situations.
- **Boosting Engagement**: By helping employees focus on the present moment, mindfulness fosters a sense of purpose and engagement with their tasks.

Practical Strategies to Integrate Mindfulness into Daily Work Routines

Mindfulness doesn't require significant time investments and can be seamlessly integrated into daily work routines:

- **Start the Day Mindfully**: Begin each workday with a brief mindfulness exercise, such as a two-minute breathing session or setting an intention for the day.

- **Mindful Task Transitions**: Pause and take a deep breath before moving from one task to another, allowing your mind to reset and refocus.
- **Desk Yoga**: Incorporate simple desk yoga poses, like seated twists or neck stretches, to relieve tension during the day.
- **Mindfulness Alarms**: Set reminders on your phone or computer to pause and practice mindfulness for a few moments throughout the day.

How Does Mindfulness Enhance Workplace Productivity?

Mindfulness improves workplace productivity by sharpening focus and decision-making:

- **Improved Focus**: Mindfulness trains the brain to avoid distractions, allowing employees to work more efficiently on their tasks.
- **Better Problem-Solving**: A calm and focused mind is more capable of generating innovative solutions and approaching challenges creatively.
- **Prioritization of Tasks**: Mindfulness encourages clarity, helping employees identify and focus on high-priority tasks rather than feeling overwhelmed by their workload.
- **Reduction of Procrastination**: Mindful awareness of habits allows employees to recognize and address procrastination tendencies, fostering better time management.

The Role of Mindful Leadership in Workplace Culture

Mindful leadership plays a pivotal role in creating a thriving and harmonious workplace:

- **Fostering Trust**: Mindful leaders cultivate trust by demonstrating empathy and active listening during conversations with their team.
- **Encouraging Inclusivity**: Practicing mindfulness enables leaders to be more aware of unconscious biases and create a more inclusive workplace culture.
- **Setting an Example**: Leaders who practice mindfulness inspire their team members to adopt similar practices, contributing to a collective sense of well-being.
- **Building Resilience**: Mindful leaders can navigate challenges with composure and provide support to their teams during difficult times.

How Can Teams Incorporate Mindfulness for Better Collaboration?

Mindfulness can strengthen teamwork by improving communication, understanding, and conflict resolution:

- **Shared Mindful Breaks**: Teams can schedule collective mindfulness breaks during meetings or long work sessions to refocus and recharge.
- **Mindful Brainstorming Sessions**: Before brainstorming, teams can engage in a short

mindfulness exercise to foster creativity and ensure everyone is fully present.

- **Creating a Mindful Workspace**: Establishing a quiet room or mindfulness corner in the office allows teams to practice mindfulness individually or collectively.
- **Celebrating Achievements Mindfully**: Teams can take a moment to acknowledge and appreciate their successes mindfully, fostering a culture of gratitude.

How Can Employees Overcome Resistance to Mindfulness at Work?

Not all employees may immediately embrace mindfulness practices. Here's how to address resistance:

- **Provide Education**: Offer workshops or training sessions to highlight the benefits of mindfulness and how it can improve work-life balance.
- **Keep It Optional**: Allow employees to opt into mindfulness activities rather than making them mandatory, ensuring they feel comfortable and unpressured.
- **Highlight Evidence-Based Benefits**: Share research or case studies demonstrating how mindfulness has improved productivity and reduced stress in similar workplaces.
- **Start Small**: Introduce mindfulness in non-intimidating ways, such as two-minute breathing exercises or mindful team check-ins.

Mindfulness and Work-Life Balance

Balancing work responsibilities with personal life is critical for well-being. Mindfulness helps achieve this balance in the following ways:

- **Detachment from Work Stress**: Practicing mindfulness during the commute home allows employees to leave work-related stress behind and transition smoothly into their personal life.
- **Mindful Scheduling**: Employees can use mindfulness to identify and prioritize both professional and personal obligations, ensuring neither is neglected.
- **Recognizing Burnout Signs**: Mindfulness fosters self-awareness, allowing individuals to identify when they need a break to maintain balance and avoid over commitment.

Long-Term Career Benefits of Mindfulness

Mindfulness not only improves immediate workplace performance but also contributes to long-term career growth:

- **Enhanced Professional Reputation**: Mindful professionals are often seen as calm, reliable, and thoughtful, traits that boost career advancement.
- **Increased Adaptability**: Mindfulness enhances resilience, making employees more capable of adapting to changes and challenges in their careers.

- **Lifelong Learning**: By fostering an open and focused mindset, mindfulness encourages continuous learning and skill development.
- **Sustainable Career Growth**: Mindfulness prevents burnout, ensuring sustained performance and job satisfaction over time.

Mindfulness and Creativity at Work

Mindfulness is a powerful catalyst for creativity and innovation in the workplace:

- **Breaking Routine Thinking**: Mindfulness encourages thinking beyond habitual patterns, allowing employees to explore new ideas and solutions.
- **Creating Mental Space**: By reducing mental clutter, mindfulness opens up space for innovative and creative thoughts to emerge.
- **Stimulating Lateral Thinking**: Mindfulness helps employees consider different perspectives and connect seemingly unrelated ideas.

Chapter 14

Mindfulness for Personal Growth

How Can Mindfulness Help in Aligning Actions with Intentions?

Mindfulness enhances the process of setting and achieving intentions by creating clarity and focus:

- **Creating Mental Clarity**: Mindfulness practices, like meditation, clear mental clutter, helping you focus on what truly matters.
- **Consistent Reminders**: Mindfulness enables you to revisit and reaffirm your intentions regularly, keeping them aligned with your goals.
- **Prioritizing Tasks**: Through mindfulness, you can identify which actions serve your intentions and eliminate distractions that hinder progress.
- **Tracking Progress**: Regular mindfulness check-ins help you assess how well your actions are aligning with your intentions, offering opportunities to adjust your approach.

How Does Self-Reflection Deepen Personal Growth?

Mindful self-reflection allows for a deeper understanding of personal experiences and promotes growth:

- **Learning from Mistakes**: Reflection offers insights into past mistakes, fostering personal improvement and resilience.
- **Recognizing Patterns**: By observing recurring thoughts or behaviors, you can identify patterns that either help or hinder your growth.

- **Clarifying Values**: Reflection helps you explore your core values, ensuring that your actions align with your authentic self.
- **Fostering Gratitude**: Reflecting on positive experiences cultivates gratitude, enhancing your emotional well-being and outlook on life.

How Can Self-Compassion Foster Resilience?

Self-compassion acts as a buffer against self-criticism, enabling resilience in the face of challenges:

- **Reducing the Fear of Failure**: By accepting mistakes with compassion, you can take risks without fear of judgment or self-blame.
- **Encouraging Self-Motivation**: Kind self-talk fosters an intrinsic desire to improve, rather than relying on external validation.
- **Building Emotional Resilience**: Self-compassion provides emotional support during difficult times, preventing feelings of overwhelm.
- **Creating a Positive Inner Voice**: Replacing harsh self-criticism with kind affirmations helps you view yourself in a more positive light, boosting confidence.

How Can We Overcome Self-Doubt Using Mindfulness?

Mindfulness provides tools to recognize and combat self-doubt:

- **Cultivating Self-Awareness**: Mindfulness allows you to observe negative self-talk without judgment, creating space to challenge it constructively.

- **Reframing Thoughts**: By identifying cognitive distortions, such as catastrophizing, you can replace them with realistic, empowering thoughts.
- **Building a Positive Feedback Loop**: Celebrating small victories reinforces your belief in your capabilities and reduces self-doubt.
- **Focusing on Progress Over Perfection**: Mindfulness encourages you to acknowledge incremental progress rather than striving for unrealistic perfection.

How Does Mindfulness Help in Embracing Life's Changes?

Mindfulness fosters adaptability and resilience during periods of change:

- **Creating Emotional Stability**: Regular mindfulness practice helps you remain calm and composed when faced with uncertainty.
- **Letting Go of Resistance**: Mindfulness enables you to accept change as a natural part of life, reducing resistance and fostering adaptability.
- **Maintaining a Present-Moment Focus**: By focusing on the present, you can release worries about the future or regrets about the past.
- **Developing a Growth Mindset**: Mindfulness strengthens your belief in your ability to learn and grow through challenges.

How Can Visualization Enhance the Effectiveness of Intentions?

Visualization is a mindfulness technique that strengthens the connection between intentions and outcomes:

- **Building Confidence**: Visualizing successful outcomes reinforces belief in your ability to achieve them.
- **Activating the Subconscious Mind**: Visualization helps implant goals into your subconscious, aligning your thoughts and actions with your intentions.
- **Identifying Obstacles**: Through visualization, you can foresee potential challenges and develop strategies to address them.
- **Boosting Motivation**: A vivid mental image of your desired outcome keeps you motivated and committed to your goals.

How Does Journaling Support Mindful Self-Reflection?

Journaling is a practical tool for self-reflection and personal growth:

- **Organizing Thoughts**: Writing helps structure and clarify your thoughts, making it easier to process your emotions.
- **Tracking Growth**: Journaling provides a record of your journey, allowing you to recognize growth and celebrate achievements.

- **Exploring Emotions**: By writing about feelings, you can identify triggers and understand your emotional responses better.
- **Setting New Goals**: Reflection through journaling often reveals new areas for personal development, keeping you focused and purposeful.

What Role Does Self-Affirmation Play in Building Confidence?

Positive affirmations reinforce a healthy self-image and build confidence:

- **Creating Positive Neural Pathways**: Repeating affirmations rewires your brain to focus on strengths rather than weaknesses.
- **Boosting Emotional Strength**: Affirmations help build resilience by instilling hope and optimism.
- **Overcoming Negative Beliefs**: Replacing self-doubt with affirmations reduces the power of limiting beliefs.
- **Strengthening Self-Worth**: Affirmations reinforce your inherent value, regardless of external achievements or failures.

How Can We Stay Flexible While Pursuing Personal Growth?

Flexibility is essential to navigate challenges and opportunities on the path of personal growth:

- **Adapting to New Goals**: Mindfulness allows you to reassess and adjust your goals based on changing circumstances or priorities.
- **Maintaining Resilience**: Flexibility fosters resilience by enabling you to bounce back from setbacks.
- **Embracing Opportunities**: Staying open-minded and adaptable allows you to seize unexpected opportunities that align with your growth.
- **Reevaluating Strategies**: Flexibility ensures that when an approach isn't working, you can pivot and explore alternative methods.

How Does Mindfulness Cultivate a Growth Mindset?

Mindfulness and a growth mindset are interconnected tools for personal transformation:

- **Encouraging Lifelong Learning**: Mindfulness fosters curiosity and a desire to learn, essential elements of a growth mindset.
- **Accepting Feedback Positively**: Mindfulness reduces defensiveness, enabling you to use feedback constructively.
- **Seeing Challenges as Opportunities**: Mindfulness shifts your perspective, allowing you to view obstacles as opportunities to grow.
- **Fostering Resilience**: With mindfulness, setbacks are seen as temporary and valuable learning experiences rather than failures.

Chapter 15

Integrating Mindfulness into Daily Life

How Can I Start a Mindfulness Practice Without Feeling Overwhelmed?

Starting a mindfulness practice can feel daunting, but taking gradual steps makes the process manageable:

- **Begin with Breathing Exercises**: Start by focusing on your breath for just one or two minutes daily. This simple practice helps anchor your mind in the present moment.
- **Incorporate Mindfulness Into Existing Habits**: Pair mindfulness with activities like brushing your teeth or drinking coffee, using these moments to practice being fully present.
- **Use Reminders**: Set reminders on your phone or leave sticky notes to prompt mindfulness practice throughout the day.
- **Celebrate Small Wins**: Acknowledge each moment you spend being mindful, as this reinforces the habit without adding pressure.

What If I Struggle to Find a Quiet Space for Mindfulness?

A quiet environment is ideal but not always necessary for mindfulness:

- **Practice Mindfulness Anywhere**: Engage in mindfulness during commutes, while waiting in line, or even in a bustling office by focusing on your breath or bodily sensations.

- **Use Noise-Canceling Tools**: Noise-canceling headphones or calming music can help create a sense of quiet even in noisy environments.
- **Transform Your Surroundings**: Add calming elements like a candle, plant, or soothing decor to a shared space to make it more conducive to mindfulness.

How Can Technology Enhance My Mindfulness Practice?

Technology can make mindfulness accessible and engaging:

- **Track Your Progress**: Many apps allow you to log your sessions, helping you stay consistent and see how far you've come.
- **Personalized Guidance**: Apps often include meditation programs tailored to specific needs, such as stress reduction or better sleep.
- **Community Connection**: Some apps offer forums and live sessions, enabling you to connect with others practicing mindfulness.
- **Timers and Bells**: Use app features like meditation timers with gentle chimes to structure your practice effectively.

How Do Mindfulness Retreats and Workshops Deepen Practice?

Retreats and workshops provide immersive experiences that enrich mindfulness practices:

- **Focused Environment**: Retreats eliminate daily distractions, allowing for deeper engagement with mindfulness techniques.
- **Expert Guidance**: Workshops often feature experienced teachers who can provide personalized feedback and techniques to refine your practice.
- **Building Resilience**: Extended periods of mindfulness during retreats enhance your ability to stay present in daily life.
- **Forming Connections**: Interacting with others in these settings fosters a sense of community and shared learning.

How Can I Share Mindfulness With My Children or Colleagues?

Sharing mindfulness with others fosters mutual growth and understanding:

- **For Children**: Introduce mindfulness through fun activities like mindful coloring, storytelling, or simple breathing games to make the practice engaging and relatable.
- **For the Workplace**: Suggest starting meetings with a one-minute mindfulness exercise or organizing short mindfulness workshops to create a more focused and collaborative environment.
- **For Friends and Community**: Host casual gatherings where mindfulness techniques are explored, such as mindful eating sessions or group meditations.

How Do I Incorporate Mindfulness Into Everyday Activities?

Mindfulness can seamlessly blend into your routine:

- **Mindful Eating**: Pay attention to the flavors, textures, and sensations of each bite, transforming meals into moments of mindfulness.
- **Mindful Walking**: Focus on the sensation of your feet touching the ground, your breathing, and the environment around you while walking.
- **Mindful Working**: Take short mindfulness breaks during tasks by pausing to observe your thoughts and refocus.
- **Mindful Chores**: Turn mundane tasks like washing dishes into mindful practices by fully engaging your senses in the process.

How Can I Maintain Consistency in My Practice?

Consistency is key to reaping the benefits of mindfulness:

- **Create a Routine**: Link mindfulness to regular activities like waking up or winding down to establish a reliable habit.
- **Stay Flexible**: Adjust the duration and timing of your practice based on your schedule to avoid feeling burdened.
- **Seek Accountability**: Practice with a friend or join a mindfulness group to stay motivated and consistent.

- **Reflect on Benefits**: Regularly remind yourself of how mindfulness positively impacts your mood, focus, and overall well-being.

What Are the Benefits of Celebrating Progress in Mindfulness?

Acknowledging milestones keeps you motivated and focused on growth:

- **Building Confidence**: Recognizing your achievements reinforces the belief in your ability to maintain mindfulness.
- **Tracking Growth**: Reflecting on progress helps you see how mindfulness has improved your life, encouraging further practice.
- **Enhancing Motivation**: Celebrating successes—no matter how small—creates a positive feedback loop, making you more likely to stick with the practice.
- **Fostering Gratitude**: Being grateful for the progress you've made enhances your sense of accomplishment and overall happiness.

How Can I Incorporate Mindfulness While Facing Challenges?

Mindfulness can be a stabilizing force during difficult times:

- **Focus on the Present**: Redirect attention from future worries or past regrets by grounding yourself in the here and now.

- **Practice Acceptance**: Acknowledge challenging emotions without judgment, allowing them to pass without overwhelming you.
- **Use the Body as an Anchor**: Focus on physical sensations, such as your breath or the feeling of your feet on the ground, to stabilize your mind.
- **Engage in Gratitude Practice**: Even in tough times, identify small things you're grateful for to shift your perspective toward positivity.

How Can a Supportive Community Strengthen Mindfulness Practice?

Being part of a mindfulness community provides encouragement and inspiration:

- **Shared Learning**: Exchanging experiences and techniques with others broadens your understanding of mindfulness.
- **Accountability**: Practicing with others keeps you consistent and motivated to show up.
- **Emotional Support**: A community offers empathy and reassurance during moments of doubt or struggle.
- **Collective Energy**: Meditating or practicing mindfulness in a group often enhances focus and creates a shared sense of purpose.

Chapter 16

The Science of Mindfulness

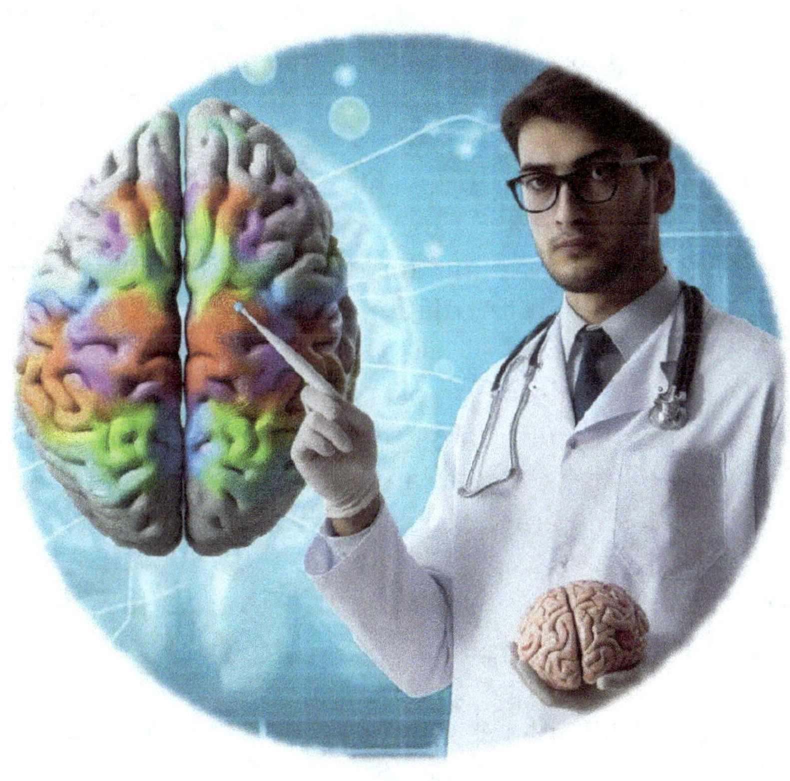

How Does Mindfulness Increase Gray Matter Volume?

Mindfulness has been shown to enhance the structure of the brain by increasing gray matter volume in key regions:

- **Hippocampus**: Regular mindfulness practice can boost the hippocampus, a brain region critical for learning and memory. This improvement can enhance memory retention and recall capabilities.
- **Amygdala**: While the amygdala is responsible for processing emotions, mindfulness practice can reduce its activity, helping to lower stress and anxiety.
- **Cingulate Cortex**: This region, associated with decision-making and empathy, benefits from increased gray matter volume, fostering better emotional regulation and interpersonal relationships.
- **How This Happens**: The repetitive focus during mindfulness meditation activates these brain areas, stimulating neuronal growth and increasing gray matter density over time.

What Specific Neural Connections Does Mindfulness Strengthen?

Mindfulness enhances communication and connectivity between various brain regions:

- **Prefrontal Cortex and Amygdala**: Strengthened connections between these areas improve emotional regulation, helping individuals respond to stress with greater resilience.

- **Hemispheric Communication**: Mindfulness fosters cross-communication between the brain's hemispheres, improving creativity, problem-solving, and holistic thinking.
- **Default Mode Network (DMN) Suppression**: By reducing DMN activity, mindfulness prevents overthinking and self-criticism, enabling a more present-focused mindset.

How Does Mindfulness Impact the Default Mode Network (DMN)?

The DMN is active when the mind is at rest, often causing unhelpful thoughts like rumination and worry:

- **Interrupting the Cycle**: Mindfulness interrupts DMN activity by redirecting attention to the present, breaking cycles of repetitive negative thinking.
- **Enhancing Present-Focused Awareness**: With less activity in the DMN, the brain can better focus on the immediate environment and tasks at hand.
- **Strengthening Task-Positive Networks**: While reducing DMN activity, mindfulness enhances task-positive networks, improving focus and productivity.

How Does Mindfulness Boost Brain Plasticity?

Mindfulness improves neuroplasticity by encouraging the growth of new neural pathways:

- **Repeated Practice**: Regular mindfulness acts as a mental exercise that strengthens neural circuits associated with attention, compassion, and emotional regulation.
- **Repairing Cognitive Damage**: For individuals recovering from trauma or neurological conditions, mindfulness helps the brain repair itself by forming alternative neural routes.
- **Long-Term Benefits**: Enhanced neuroplasticity translates to better adaptability, resilience, and an overall sense of well-being.

How Does Mindfulness Support the Immune System?

Mindfulness positively influences the immune system in several ways:

- **Reducing Inflammation**: Chronic stress increases inflammation, weakening immunity. Mindfulness lowers stress levels, reducing inflammatory markers in the body.
- **Boosting Antibody Production**: Studies suggest mindfulness practices like meditation can enhance the production of antibodies, improving the body's ability to fight infections.
- **Improving Sleep Quality**: Better sleep, often a result of mindfulness, strengthens immune

defenses' by allowing the body to repair and regenerate.

- **Balancing the Nervous System**: Mindfulness activates the parasympathetic nervous system, known as the "rest-and-digest" system, enhancing immune response.

What Role Does Cortisol Play, and How Does Mindfulness Regulate It?

Cortisol, the primary stress hormone, can disrupt health when levels are consistently high:

- **Regulating the HPA Axis**: Mindfulness helps regulate the hypothalamic-pituitary-adrenal (HPA) axis, which controls cortisol release. A balanced HPA axis leads to healthier stress responses.
- **Lowering Chronic Stress Levels**: By reducing stress, mindfulness prevents prolonged cortisol elevation, which can otherwise impair immune function, disrupt sleep, and contribute to weight gain.
- **Promoting Emotional Stability**: Lower cortisol levels lead to better emotional balance, reducing the intensity of negative reactions to daily stressors.

How Does Mindfulness Influence Telomere Length?

Telomeres, protective caps at the ends of chromosomes, are crucial for cellular health and longevity:

- **Stress Reduction and Telomeres**: Chronic stress accelerates telomere shortening. Mindfulness reduces stress, potentially slowing this process and promoting healthier aging.
- **Activation of Enzymes**: Mindfulness increases the activity of telomerase, an enzyme that helps maintain telomere length, thus supporting cellular health.
- **Research Findings**: Studies show that mindfulness practitioners often have longer telomeres compared to non-practitioners, indicating a slower aging process and reduced risk of age-related diseases.

What Are the Holistic Health Benefits of Mindfulness?

In addition to its neuroscientific benefits, mindfulness positively affects overall health:

- **Heart Health**: Mindfulness lowers blood pressure and improves cardiovascular health by reducing stress and promoting relaxation.
- **Digestive Health**: The calming effects of mindfulness enhance digestion by activating the parasympathetic nervous system.
- **Mental Health**: Regular practice reduces symptoms of depression and anxiety, fostering a more balanced and positive outlook.
- **Enhanced Focus and Productivity**: By improving attention and reducing mental distractions, mindfulness increases efficiency in both professional and personal tasks.

How Can Science-Based Mindfulness Practices Be Applied in Daily Life?

To incorporate scientific mindfulness into your routine:

- **Focused Attention Practices**: Dedicate a few minutes daily to focus on your breath or a specific sensation, strengthening brain regions linked to mindfulness.
- **Mindful Movement**: Activities like yoga or tai chi incorporate mindful awareness with physical movement, benefiting both the mind and body.
- **Guided Meditations**: Use technology or mindfulness groups to access scientifically backed meditations tailored to specific health or cognitive goals.

Chapter 17

Overcoming Challenges in Mindfulness Practice

Why Does the Mind Wander During Mindfulness Practice?

Mind wandering is a natural aspect of human cognition.

- **Default Mode Network (DMN)**: This brain network is responsible for daydreaming and self-referential thinking, which often leads to wandering thoughts.
- **Habitual Thinking Patterns**: The mind is conditioned to constantly analyze, plan, or worry. Breaking these patterns requires practice.
- **Strategies to Address Wandering**:

  1. Accept wandering as a natural occurrence. Instead of resisting it, acknowledge the thought and gently guide your focus back to the present.
  2. Use a mantra or a specific anchor like the breath or a sensation to keep your mind engaged.

How Can You Manage Restlessness or Physical Discomfort During Practice?

Restlessness or discomfort is common, especially for beginners:

- **Adjust Your Position**: Experiment with different postures—sitting on a cushion, chair, or lying down—to find one that minimizes discomfort.

- **Incorporate Movement**: Practices like mindful walking or yoga allow for mindfulness while reducing physical restlessness.
- **Engage in Pre-Meditation Stretches**: Gentle stretches before mindfulness sessions can help release tension in the body.
- **Shift Your Focus**: Instead of resisting discomfort, focus on the sensation itself. Observe it with curiosity, noting how it changes over time.

Why Do Some People Experience Frustration with Mindfulness?

Frustration often arises from unmet expectations or difficulty staying focused:

- **Reframe Your Goals**: Mindfulness is about the process, not achieving a specific state. Shift focus from results to the practice itself.
- **Acknowledge Progress**: Recognize small successes, like noticing your wandering mind and bringing it back to focus.
- **Use Guided Practices**: Apps and recordings with step-by-step instructions can help reduce frustration by providing clear guidance.

How Can People Incorporate Mindfulness Into a Busy Schedule?

Finding time for mindfulness in a packed day is challenging but achievable:

- **Start Small**: Even 1-2 minutes of mindfulness can make a difference. Short practices like mindful breathing can fit into busy schedules.
- **Combine With Daily Activities**: Practice mindfulness while brushing your teeth, eating, or walking. Focus on the sensations and experience of the activity.
- **Use Breaks Effectively**: Turn work or study breaks into mindfulness moments by stepping away from distractions and centering your attention.
- **Schedule It**: Treat mindfulness as an important meeting with yourself. Add it to your calendar to create accountability.

What Can You Do When Self-Doubt Interferes With Practice?

Self-doubt can hinder mindfulness, but it can be addressed:

- **Recognize It as a Thought**: View self-doubt as just another mental event. Observe it without judgment and let it pass.
- **Celebrate Small Wins**: Acknowledge every moment of focus, no matter how brief, as progress.
- **Seek Encouragement**: Join a mindfulness group or read about others' experiences to remind yourself that challenges are normal.
- **Practice Self-Compassion**: Use affirmations or compassionate phrases like, "It's okay to struggle. I'm learning."

What Are Some Additional Tips for Handling Distractions?

Distractions are inevitable, but they can be managed effectively:

- **Visualize Boundaries**: Imagine a protective bubble around your practice space to mentally block out external disturbances.
- **Use White Noise**: Background sounds like rain or ocean waves can mask disruptive noises and create a calming environment.
- **Minimize Interruptions**: Communicate with family or housemates about your mindfulness time to avoid interruptions.
- **Observe the Distraction**: Instead of resisting, briefly observe the distraction with curiosity, then bring your focus back.

How Can You Stay Consistent With Mindfulness Practice Over Time?

Consistency is key to mindfulness, and building a habit requires:

- **Habit Stacking**: Link mindfulness practice to an existing habit, like meditating right after brushing your teeth.
- **Use Reminders**: Set alarms or place visual cues (like a meditation cushion) to remind you to practice.
- **Reward Yourself**: Celebrate milestones, such as completing a week of practice, with small rewards.

- **Reflect on Benefits**: Regularly remind yourself of the improvements mindfulness has brought to your life, such as reduced stress or improved focus.

When Should You Consider Seeking Professional Guidance?

Professional guidance can help when you face persistent challenges:

- **Personalized Feedback**: A mindfulness teacher or coach can offer tailored advice and help identify areas for improvement.
- **Overcoming Plateaus**: If your practice feels stagnant, guidance from an expert can provide new techniques and perspectives.
- **Addressing Emotional Challenges**: Mindfulness can bring up deep emotions. A therapist trained in mindfulness-based interventions can provide support.
- **Deepening Your Practice**: Attending a retreat or workshop allows for immersive learning and dedicated time to refine skills.

How Can You Build a Support System for Your Practice?

Connecting with others can enhance your mindfulness journey:

- **Find an Accountability Partner**: Share your goals with a friend who also practices mindfulness to keep each other motivated.

- **Join Online Communities**: Participate in forums or social media groups focused on mindfulness for inspiration and advice.
- **Attend Group Sessions**: Practicing with a group provides a sense of shared purpose and learning opportunities from others' experiences.

Chapter 18

Mindfulness for Specific Challenges

How Does Mindful Breathing Calm Anxiety and Panic Attacks?

Mindful breathing plays a crucial role in reducing anxiety by directly influencing the body's physiological responses:

- **Activating the Parasympathetic Nervous System**: Deep, slow breaths signal the brain to activate the "rest-and-digest" response, counteracting the fight-or-flight state associated with anxiety.
- **Stabilizing Heart Rate**: Rhythmic breathing helps stabilize heart rate, promoting a sense of calm.
- **Promoting Present-Moment Awareness**: Focusing on the breath anchors the mind in the present, reducing the overwhelming nature of anxious thoughts.

What Makes Mindful Grounding Effective for Panic Attacks?

Grounding techniques shift focus away from racing thoughts by engaging the senses:

- **Five Senses Method**: Identify five things you can see, four you can touch, three you can hear, two you can smell, and one you can taste.
- **Tactile Anchors**: Holding an object, like a smooth stone, and concentrating on its texture helps ground you in reality.

- **Physical Connection**: Feeling your feet firmly on the ground provides a reassuring sense of stability and control.

How Can Mindfulness Address Negative Thought Patterns in Depression?

Mindfulness disrupts cycles of rumination common in depression:

- **Decentering Thoughts**: Viewing negative thoughts as transient mental events rather than absolute truths reduces their power.
- **Mindful Journaling**: Writing about thoughts and emotions in a nonjudgmental way helps increase self-awareness and emotional clarity.
- **Fostering Gratitude**: Practicing mindful gratitude by noting small positive experiences encourages a shift towards more optimistic thinking.

Why Is Mindful Movement Helpful for Emotional Well-Being?

Mindful movement, like yoga or walking, combines physical activity with present-moment awareness:

- **Boosting Endorphins**: Physical activity releases endorphins, natural mood enhancers that alleviate depressive symptoms.
- **Enhancing Body Awareness**: Focusing on bodily sensations promotes a stronger mind-body connection, aiding emotional regulation.

- **Creating Rituals**: Incorporating mindful movement into daily routines provides a structured, uplifting habit.

How Does Mindfulness Help in Overcoming Addiction?

Mindfulness equips individuals with tools to navigate the challenges of addiction recovery:

- **Observing Cravings**: Mindful awareness allows individuals to observe cravings without acting on them, reducing impulsive behaviors.
- **Reducing Emotional Triggers**: Mindfulness helps identify and manage emotions that contribute to substance use, such as stress or sadness.
- **Fostering Self-Control**: Practicing mindfulness enhances emotional resilience, helping individuals resist temptations more effectively.

What Are Practical Strategies for Mindful Relapse Prevention?

Mindfulness aids in identifying and managing relapse triggers:

- **Trigger Awareness**: Maintaining a mindfulness journal to note potential triggers and emotional states.
- **Urge Surfing**: Visualize cravings as waves that rise, peak, and eventually fade, reinforcing the idea that cravings are temporary.

- **Mindful Reframing**: Shift thoughts about cravings from "I can't handle this" to "This feeling will pass."

How Does Mindfulness Reduce the Perception of Chronic Pain?

Mindfulness alters the brain's response to pain signals, offering relief:

- **Changing Pain Perception**: By observing pain nonjudgmentally, mindfulness reduces the emotional intensity associated with it.
- **Engaging Neuroplasticity**: Regular mindfulness practice fosters brain changes that decrease pain sensitivity over time.
- **Enhancing Coping Strategies**: Techniques like body scan meditations teach individuals to acknowledge pain without letting it dominate their experience.

How Can Mindful Practices Be Incorporated Into Daily Pain Management?

Mindfulness can be seamlessly integrated into routines:

- **Mindful Posture Checks**: Regularly check and adjust your posture to relieve tension.
- **Mindful Rest Periods**: Set aside moments to focus on your breathing and sensations during the day.

- **Mindful Gratitude**: Acknowledge parts of your body that feel good, shifting focus from areas of pain.

How Does Mindfulness Support the Grieving Process?

Mindfulness offers tools to navigate the complexities of grief:

- **Allowing Space for Emotions**: Mindfulness encourages embracing grief without judgment, fostering healing.
- **Creating Meaningful Rituals**: Practices like lighting a candle or mindful reflection on a loved one's life provide solace and connection.
- **Releasing Guilt**: Mindful self-compassion helps address feelings of guilt or "what-ifs" often associated with loss.

What Are Effective Mindfulness Techniques for Connecting With Positive Memories During Grief?

Focusing on cherished memories can bring comfort during grief:

- **Mindful Photo Viewing**: Spend time observing photos of your loved one, noting the emotions and stories they evoke.
- **Guided Gratitude Reflections**: Reflect on moments of joy shared with your loved one, expressing gratitude for those experiences.

- **Mindful Storytelling**: Share positive memories with others, focusing on the emotions and details of those moments.

Chapter 19

Mindfulness and Spirituality

How Can Mindfulness Enhance Spiritual Practices Across Different Religions?

Mindfulness serves as a bridge, enriching spiritual traditions by deepening self-awareness and promoting focused engagement:

- **Christian Mindfulness**: Incorporating mindfulness into contemplative prayer can enhance one's connection to scripture and God. For example, focusing on a passage from the Bible during meditation allows for deeper reflection and spiritual insight.
- **Islamic Mindfulness**: Mindful prayer (Salah) helps Muslims connect their physical actions and intentions with a sense of divine presence. Reflection and gratitude align with the spiritual discipline of Tazkiyah (self-purification).
- **Jewish Mindfulness**: Practices like Kabbalistic meditation foster introspection and spiritual growth. Regular mindfulness during daily blessings can amplify gratitude and connection to God.
- **Hindu Mindfulness**: Combining mindfulness with yoga and meditation aligns body, mind, and spirit. Practices like mantra chanting serve as a powerful focus for mindfulness, enhancing spiritual awareness.

What Are the Benefits of a Secular Mindfulness Approach for Spiritual Growth?

Secular mindfulness provides a flexible framework for individuals seeking spiritual growth without adhering to religious traditions:

- **Fostering Inner Peace**: Secular mindfulness emphasizes reducing stress and cultivating tranquility, a cornerstone of many spiritual practices.
- **Encouraging Reflection**: It provides tools for self-reflection, helping individuals connect with their inner values and purpose.
- **Promoting Inclusivity**: Without the constraints of religious doctrine, secular mindfulness can be adapted to align with personal beliefs, making spiritual exploration accessible to all.

How Does Mindfulness Cultivate Inner Peace and Compassion in Spirituality?

Mindfulness enhances core spiritual values like inner peace and compassion:

- **Reducing Judgment**: Mindfulness teaches non-judgmental awareness, helping individuals approach themselves and others with kindness.
- **Empathy Development**: By focusing on others' experiences with mindfulness, one can cultivate deeper empathy and understanding, essential for spiritual growth.

- **Peaceful Acceptance**: Mindfulness fosters acceptance of life's challenges, nurturing a resilient and tranquil spirit.

How Can We Create a Sacred Space for Mindfulness and Spirituality?

Designing a dedicated space can enhance the depth and consistency of practice:

- **Physical Setup**: A serene corner with minimal distractions, adorned with meaningful objects like candles, plants, or religious symbols, creates a calming environment.
- **Symbolic Anchors**: Items like a prayer mat, journal, or mantra card can anchor the practice and foster a sense of sacredness.
- **Regular Use**: Engaging with the space regularly reinforces the habit and deepens its personal significance.

How Does Mindfulness Help Discover Meaning and Purpose in Life?

Mindfulness nurtures a deeper sense of purpose by aligning actions with personal values:

- **Clarity Through Reflection**: Regular mindfulness practice helps identify core values, providing a roadmap for meaningful living.
- **Enhanced Gratitude**: By focusing on present blessings, mindfulness shifts the perspective from scarcity to abundance, fostering contentment.

- **Connection to Nature**: Mindful immersion in natural settings fosters a profound appreciation for life's interconnectedness, enhancing one's sense of purpose.

What Role Does Gratitude Play in Mindfulness and Spiritual Practices?

Gratitude is a transformative aspect of mindfulness and spirituality:

- **Amplifying Positive Emotions**: Practicing gratitude increases joy and reduces stress, enhancing overall well-being.
- **Strengthening Relationships**: Expressing gratitude deepens connections with others, reflecting spiritual values like kindness and reciprocity.
- **Encouraging Contentment**: Gratitude helps individuals focus on what they have rather than what they lack, promoting spiritual growth.

How Can Serving Others Enhance Both Mindfulness and Spirituality?

Acts of service integrate mindfulness and spirituality by fostering compassion and connection:

- **Mindful Volunteering**: Approaching service with full attention and care enriches the experience for both giver and receiver.
- **Developing Humility**: Serving others reminds individuals of their role within the greater whole, reinforcing spiritual humility.

- **Fostering Community**: Engaging in service builds a sense of belonging and shared purpose, deepening spiritual ties.

How Does Mindfulness in the Present Moment Deepen Spiritual Awareness?

Being present fosters spiritual connection by encouraging acceptance and clarity:

- **Letting Go of Regret and Worry**: Mindfulness reduces the hold of past regrets and future anxieties, paving the way for spiritual serenity.
- **Experiencing Divine Presence**: Focusing on the now heightens awareness of the sacredness embedded in daily life.
- **Heightening Intuition**: A clear and present mind often perceives subtle spiritual insights and synchronicities.

Chapter 20

The Future of Mindfulness

How Can Mindfulness Be Effectively Integrated into Educational Settings?

Incorporating mindfulness into schools can create a supportive environment for learning, emotional well-being, and personal growth:

- **Mindful Classroom Practices**: Teachers can start the day with brief mindfulness exercises, such as guided breathing or visualizations, to help students focus and prepare for learning.
- **Tailored Interventions**: Programs like "Mindful Schools" offer age-appropriate mindfulness curricula designed to meet students' developmental needs.
- **Parental Involvement**: Encouraging parents to practice mindfulness at home reinforces its benefits for children.
- **Addressing Special Needs**: Mindfulness strategies, such as body scans or grounding techniques, can help students with ADHD or sensory sensitivities manage their challenges.

What Are the Benefits of Mindfulness in Healthcare Beyond Stress Reduction?

Mindfulness supports physical and emotional health in a variety of ways:

- **Boosting Immunity**: Studies suggest that mindfulness practices can enhance immune function, reducing susceptibility to illness.

- **Managing Chronic Illness**: Beyond pain management, mindfulness helps individuals with conditions like diabetes, heart disease, or autoimmune disorders by improving self-care habits and reducing stress-induced symptoms.
- **Emotional Resilience**: Mindfulness aids in processing difficult emotions, making it a valuable tool for those coping with serious diagnoses or grief.
- **Patient-Provider Relationships**: Encouraging healthcare providers to practice mindfulness can lead to improved empathy, communication, and patient satisfaction.

How Can Mindfulness Transform the Workplace Culture?

Mindfulness is more than an individual practice; it can reshape how organizations function:

- **Improving Workplace Wellness**: Mindfulness programs can reduce employee burnout, absenteeism, and turnover, leading to a healthier workforce.
- **Enhancing Creativity and Innovation**: Mindfulness helps employees tap into creative thinking by reducing mental clutter and fostering openness to new ideas.
- **Mindful Decision-Making**: Leaders trained in mindfulness are better equipped to make thoughtful, balanced decisions that align with organizational goals.

- **Cultivating Inclusive Environments**: Mindfulness fosters understanding and respect among diverse teams, enhancing inclusivity and collaboration.

What Role Do Technology and Apps Play in the Global Mindfulness Movement?

Technology has democratized access to mindfulness, making it easier for individuals to practice and learn:

- **Customized Experiences**: Apps like Headspace and Calm offer tailored meditation plans based on user preferences and goals.
- **Data-Driven Insights**: Wearables with mindfulness features, such as heart rate monitoring during meditation, provide real-time feedback to enhance practice.
- **Global Reach**: Online mindfulness workshops and virtual retreats allow participants from around the world to engage in shared learning experiences.
- **AI Integration**: Future mindfulness apps may incorporate AI to deliver highly personalized meditation guidance and support.

What Are the Key Trends Driving the Global Mindfulness Movement?

The mindfulness movement is expanding due to increasing societal awareness and demand:

- **Institutional Adoption**: Schools, healthcare facilities, and corporations are integrating mindfulness into their standard practices.
- **Cross-Cultural Adaptation**: Mindfulness practices are being tailored to different cultural contexts, making them more accessible globally.
- **Celebrity Advocacy**: Public figures and influencers are raising awareness of mindfulness, promoting its benefits to broader audiences.
- **Collaborative Research**: Academic institutions worldwide are collaborating to study the multifaceted benefits of mindfulness, fostering innovation.

What Does Current Research Reveal About Mindfulness and Brain Health?

Neuroscience is shedding light on the transformative effects of mindfulness:

- **Neuroplasticity**: Mindfulness practices encourage the brain to rewire itself, strengthening areas related to focus, empathy, and emotional regulation.
- **Stress Reduction at the Neural Level**: Mindfulness decreases activity in the amygdala, reducing stress responses and enhancing emotional stability.
- **Improved Memory and Learning**: By enhancing the hippocampus's function, mindfulness supports better memory retention and cognitive flexibility.

- **Slowing Cognitive Decline**: Emerging research suggests mindfulness can delay age-related cognitive decline, providing benefits for older adults.

How Can Mindfulness Be Adapted for Specific Populations?

Mindfulness can be tailored to suit the unique needs of diverse groups:

- **Children and Adolescents**: Introducing mindfulness through playful activities, such as mindful coloring or nature walks, makes it accessible and engaging for younger audiences.
- **Older Adults**: Practices focused on balance, gentle movement, and memory support can cater to aging populations.
- **Individuals with Trauma**: Trauma-sensitive mindfulness incorporates grounding techniques and prioritizes safety, helping participants avoid retraumatization.
- **Underserved Communities**: Free or low-cost mindfulness programs delivered through community centers or online platforms ensure inclusivity.

What Are the Promising Areas for Future Mindfulness Research?

As mindfulness gains mainstream acceptance, researchers are exploring new frontiers:

- **Epigenetics**: Investigating how mindfulness influences gene expression related to stress and resilience.
- **Mindfulness in Virtual Reality (VR)**: Using VR to create immersive environments for mindfulness practice, enhancing its effectiveness.
- **Global Health Applications**: Developing mindfulness interventions to address global health challenges like pandemic-induced stress or climate anxiety.
- **Integration with Artificial Intelligence**: Harnessing AI to deliver personalized mindfulness support based on real-time data and individual preferences.

Chapter 21

The Mindful Journey: A Personal Reflection

How Can I Track My Progress in Mindfulness Practice?

Tracking your mindfulness journey ensures that you recognize growth while identifying areas for improvement:

- **Journaling**: Keep a mindfulness journal where you reflect on your daily or weekly practice, noting challenges, insights, and successes.
- **Mindfulness Assessments**: Use tools like the Mindful Attention Awareness Scale (MAAS) to gauge your progress.
- **Feedback from Peers**: Share your journey with a mindfulness group or mentor to gain valuable external perspectives.
- **Revisiting Challenges**: Periodically assess how previously challenging situations now feel more manageable due to your practice.

What Are Creative Ways to Share Mindfulness with Others?

Engaging others in mindfulness can be inspiring and fulfilling:

- **Mindful Storytelling**: Share personal stories of transformation to inspire others to embark on their mindfulness journey.
- **Art and Creativity**: Use mediums like painting, poetry, or music to express the essence of mindfulness and connect with others.

- **Mindfulness in Family Gatherings**: Introduce simple practices like gratitude exercises or mindful meals during family events.
- **Social Media Advocacy**: Share mindfulness tips, experiences, and resources on platforms to reach a broader audience.

How Can I Overcome Plateaus or Stagnation in My Practice?

It's natural to experience periods of stagnation in mindfulness practice. Here's how to reignite progress:

- **Explore New Techniques**: Try advanced practices like loving-kindness meditation, body scans, or mindful walking.
- **Join Advanced Retreats**: Participate in mindfulness retreats designed to deepen practice and provide fresh insights.
- **Revisit Your Intentions**: Reflect on why you started practicing mindfulness and renew your commitment.
- **Incorporate Daily Life Activities**: Practice mindfulness during routine tasks, such as cooking, cleaning, or commuting, to bring novelty to your routine.

What Does a Mindful Workplace Look Like?

A workplace grounded in mindfulness offers benefits for employees and organizations alike:

- **Mindful Meetings**: Begin meetings with a moment of silence to focus and foster presence.

- **Stress Management Programs**: Offer mindfulness-based stress reduction (MBSR) workshops to employees.
- **Work-Life Balance Initiatives**: Encourage mindfulness practices that help employees detach from work after hours.
- **Leadership Training**: Teach mindful leadership to help managers cultivate empathy, clarity, and thoughtful decision-making.

How Can Technology Support My Mindfulness Practice Without Creating Distractions?

Technology can enhance mindfulness while ensuring it doesn't detract from the practice:

- **Dedicated Apps**: Use apps like Insight Timer or Calm, which focus solely on mindfulness and meditation.
- **Wearables for Tracking**: Devices like smartwatches with mindfulness features help monitor stress levels and remind you to pause.
- **Mindful Notifications**: Set reminders on your devices to take breaks for mindful breathing or stretching.
- **Digital Detox Periods**: Balance technology use by scheduling screen-free times to deepen your practice.

How Can I Cultivate Long-Term Mindfulness Goals?

Building mindfulness as a lifelong habit requires sustained effort and intention:

- **Vision Statements**: Create a personal mindfulness vision, such as "Living each moment with purpose and presence."
- **Setting Milestones**: Break your goals into short-term (daily), medium-term (monthly), and long-term (yearly) milestones.
- **Ongoing Education**: Continue learning through books, workshops, and advanced courses to keep your practice evolving.
- **Intergenerational Sharing**: Pass mindfulness traditions to younger generations through storytelling and shared practices.

How Does the Future of Mindfulness Align with Societal Trends?

Mindfulness is adapting to contemporary needs, and its integration into society is poised for growth:

- **AI and Mindfulness**: Emerging AI technologies can provide real-time feedback and personalized guidance during mindfulness sessions.
- **Workplace Culture Shifts**: Companies are recognizing mindfulness as a core strategy for employee well-being and productivity.
- **Mindfulness and Diversity**: Tailoring mindfulness programs to various cultural and

socioeconomic contexts ensures accessibility for all communities.

- **Global Collaborative Efforts**: International organizations are fostering mindfulness research and implementation across education, healthcare, and public policy.

How Can I Make Mindfulness a Family Practice?

Integrating mindfulness into family life creates a nurturing environment for all members:

- **Family Gratitude Circles**: Share daily moments of gratitude during meals or before bedtime.
- **Mindful Playtime**: Engage in activities like yoga or nature walks that encourage mindfulness together.
- **Modeling Behavior**: Practice mindfulness openly, setting an example for younger family members.
- **Storytime Meditation**: Incorporate simple breathing exercises or visualization stories before bedtime to instill mindfulness habits in children

Chapter 22

Mindfulness and Creativity

How Does Mindfulness Enhance the Creative Process?

Mindfulness can significantly enhance the creative process by fostering a conducive environment for innovation:

- **Mindful Preparation**: Creating a calm and inspiring environment primes your mind for creativity. This could mean decluttering your workspace, playing calming music, or simply sitting quietly to set the tone before beginning a creative task.
- **Mindful Generation**: Use mindfulness techniques such as brainstorming, mind mapping, and free writing to allow your ideas to flow freely. These practices reduce judgment and encourage creative thinking by letting your mind wander without constraint.
- **Mindful Evaluation**: Take a step back from your work and evaluate your ideas objectively. Mindfulness helps you assess ideas without the pressure of urgency, enabling a more balanced approach to decision-making. It helps in prioritizing ideas that align with your vision and goals.
- **Mindful Execution**: Focus on one task at a time. Multitasking can dilute your energy and focus, but mindfulness encourages single-tasking, which allows you to pour your attention into completing each task effectively.
- **Mindful Reflection**: After completing a task or creative process, take time to reflect on what

worked well and what didn't. This reflection is a key aspect of mindfulness, helping you learn from your experiences and improving your creative approach over time.

What Are Effective Strategies to Overcome Creative Blocks Using Mindfulness?

Creative blocks are common and can be frustrating, but mindfulness provides tools to overcome them:

- **Reducing Stress and Anxiety**: Mindfulness techniques like deep breathing exercises, body scans, and meditation can help calm the mind and reduce anxiety. When stress is managed, you're more likely to approach creative tasks with a relaxed and open attitude.
- **Improving Focus and Concentration**: Regular mindfulness practice enhances concentration by training the mind to stay present. This helps in keeping distractions at bay and improves your ability to focus on your creative task.
- **Enhancing Emotional Intelligence**: Mindfulness allows you to recognize and manage your emotions more effectively. Understanding your feelings can lead to better emotional regulation and a more positive outlook, which is crucial when facing creative challenges.
- **Cultivating a Positive Mindset**: By practicing mindfulness, you develop a more optimistic mindset. This encourages a willingness to experiment and take risks, which are essential traits for creativity and innovation.

How Does Mindfulness Foster Innovation?

Innovation often requires creative problem-solving and thinking outside the box. Mindfulness can facilitate this process:

- **Open-Mindedness**: Mindfulness encourages a state of openness where you're not constrained by preconceptions or habitual thinking. This allows you to consider new ideas and perspectives without judgment.
- **Flexible Thinking**: A mindful state supports flexible thinking, which is essential for adapting to new information or changing circumstances. Mindfulness teaches you to view problems from multiple angles and find solutions that might not be immediately apparent.
- **Problem-Solving**: By approaching problems with a clear, focused mind, mindfulness helps you identify innovative solutions. It prevents the mind from being cluttered with extraneous details and allows you to think strategically about challenges.

How Can Mindfulness Be Incorporated into the Creative Practice?

Integrating mindfulness into your creative practice can unlock your full potential:

- **Mindful Work Environment**: Establish a workspace that supports mindfulness, with minimal distractions and tools that facilitate focus and relaxation. This could include plants, natural light, or art that inspires creativity.

- **Mindful Techniques**: Use mindfulness exercises specifically designed for creativity, such as mindful drawing or painting, mindful writing, or mindful movement exercises. These techniques help tap into your subconscious and encourage creative flow.

- **Mindful Collaboration**: If working with others, encourage a mindful approach to brainstorming and collaboration. This means being present in discussions, listening without judgment, and fostering an environment where all ideas are welcomed.

- **Practice Regularly**: Like any other skill, mindfulness requires regular practice. Make it a habit to integrate mindfulness into your daily routine, whether it's through dedicated meditation sessions or simply taking a mindful pause throughout your day.

Chapter 23

Mindfulness and Technology

How Can We Use Technology Mindfully?

Navigating the digital age requires a thoughtful approach to using technology to support well-being rather than detract from it:

- **Mindful Social Media**: Social media can contribute to stress and distraction if not used mindfully. Be aware of how much time you spend on platforms and consider setting limits. Engage mindfully by choosing to participate in conversations that contribute positively to your mental health and well-being, and avoid mindless scrolling.
- **Digital Detox**: Taking regular breaks from technology—such as turning off notifications, scheduling device-free hours, or taking tech vacations—can significantly reduce stress levels and improve focus. A digital detox helps reclaim time for mindfulness practices, creative thinking, and relaxation.
- **Mindful Emailing**: Managing emails mindfully involves prioritizing them and avoiding multitasking while checking your inbox. Set specific times to read and respond to emails, and resist the urge to switch tasks frequently. This helps maintain focus and productivity.
- **Mindful Gaming**: Video games can be a source of stress if they lead to excessive play or distractions. By practicing mindfulness while gaming—such as focusing on the experience, appreciating the visual design, and setting time limits—you can enjoy the activity without it taking over your life.

What Are Some Mindfulness Apps and Wearables That Can Enhance the Practice?

There are several tools and apps available to support a mindful technology use:

- **Meditation Apps**: Apps like Headspace, Calm, Insight Timer, and others offer guided meditation sessions to help users develop mindfulness. These resources provide structured guidance, whether you're a beginner or looking to deepen your practice.

- **Mindfulness Wearables**: Devices like the Muse headband or Fitbit's mindfulness trackers can monitor your mental state and offer biofeedback to help you improve focus and reduce stress. These wearables can track your heart rate, brain waves, and other physiological indicators to provide personalized insights into your mindfulness practice.

- **Mindful Productivity Apps**: There are numerous apps designed to boost productivity by reducing distractions and managing time effectively. Tools like Forest, Focus@Will, and Todoist can help you stay organized, set priorities, and create a more focused work environment.

How Should We Approach Artificial Intelligence with Mindfulness?

AI technology offers numerous benefits, but it also requires a mindful approach to ensure it aligns with ethical standards and human well-being:

- **Mindful AI Design**: When designing AI systems, it's essential to prioritize human well-being. This includes considering the ethical implications of AI use, ensuring transparency, and focusing on responsible data use. Mindful AI design seeks to create tools that enhance our lives without creating dependencies or ethical dilemmas.
- **Mindful AI Use**: Using AI tools mindfully means being aware of their impact on your life and maintaining control over their use. It's important to avoid becoming overly reliant on AI and to balance their use with human intuition, creativity, and judgment.

What Can We Expect in the Future of Mindfulness and Technology?

The future of mindfulness and technology is promising, with continuous innovations that integrate mindfulness practices into our daily lives:

- **Virtual and Augmented Reality Mindfulness Experiences**: Technologies like VR and AR can offer immersive mindfulness experiences that transport you to tranquil environments, helping you relax and de-stress in a way that's not possible with traditional media.
- **AI-Powered Mindfulness Coaches**: Artificial intelligence can assist in providing personalized mindfulness guidance, adapting to individual needs and preferences. These coaches can offer

tailored recommendations for meditation, stress reduction, and overall well-being.

- **Mindful Robotics**: As robots become more integrated into our lives, they can serve as companions and assist with mindfulness practices. These robots could provide companionship, engage in mindfulness exercises, or simply offer reminders to stay present.

Chapter 24

Mindfulness and the Environment

How Can We Apply Mindfulness to Our Relationship with the Environment?

Mindfulness can guide us to be more conscious of our actions and their impact on the planet. By developing a mindful awareness, we can make sustainable choices and contribute positively to the environment.

What is Conscious Consumerism?

Conscious consumerism involves making informed choices about the products we buy. It means considering their environmental footprint—such as their production processes, materials, and packaging—and opting for items that are sustainable, ethically produced, and have minimal negative impact on the environment. This includes:

- **Reduce, Reuse, Recycle**: By minimizing waste through careful consumption and recycling, we conserve resources and reduce our environmental footprint. Simple practices like buying in bulk, choosing products with less packaging, and recycling can significantly contribute to waste reduction.
- **Support Sustainable Businesses**: Supporting businesses that prioritize sustainability is crucial. This includes choosing brands that use eco-friendly materials, pay fair wages, and take responsibility for their environmental impact.

What Are Mindful Food Choices?

Mindful eating involves being conscious of the food we consume, opting for sustainable options that benefit both our health and the environment:

- **Mindful Food Choices**: This means choosing foods that are organic, local, and sustainably sourced. Reducing meat consumption and increasing plant-based options can lower greenhouse gas emissions associated with food production.
- **Reduce Food Waste**: By planning meals, storing food properly, and composting food scraps, we can minimize waste and support a more sustainable food system. Composting organic waste helps improve soil quality and reduce methane emissions from landfills.
- **Support Local Farmers**: Buying from local farmers reduces the carbon footprint associated with long-distance transportation and supports local economies.

How Can We Integrate Mindfulness into Our Transportation Choices?

Choosing sustainable transportation options is another way to practice mindfulness regarding our environmental impact:

- **Mindful Transportation**: Opt for walking, biking, carpooling, or public transit over driving alone. These choices not only reduce carbon emissions but also encourage physical activity and community interaction.

- **Support Sustainable Businesses**: Prefer businesses that offer eco-friendly transportation options or work with partners who implement green practices. This could include companies that provide electric vehicles, bike-friendly infrastructure, or incentives for sustainable commuting.

What is Mindful Living in the Context of Home and Environment?

Creating a mindful living space is about fostering a sustainable and harmonious environment at home:

- **Mindful Home Design**: This involves using eco-friendly building materials, energy-efficient appliances, and thoughtful interior design that promotes comfort and reduces environmental impact. Incorporating natural light, using low-VOC paints, and choosing sustainable furniture can enhance the overall well-being of the living space.

- **Mindful Cleaning**: Cleaning your home with eco-friendly products that do not harm the environment or indoor air quality is essential. This can include using reusable cleaning cloths, vinegar, and baking soda as natural alternatives to harsh chemicals.

- **Mindful Gardening**: Engage with nature through gardening, which can contribute positively to biodiversity and soil health. Growing your own fruits, vegetables, and herbs supports sustainable food practices and reduces your carbon footprint.

How Can Mindfulness Help Manage Eco-Anxiety?

Mindfulness can be a valuable tool for managing anxiety related to environmental issues like climate change:

- **Climate Action**: By practicing mindfulness, you can focus on what you can do to make a difference. This might include reducing energy consumption, supporting renewable energy initiatives, or participating in local environmental projects.
- **Mindful Consumption**: Make conscious decisions about the products you buy and the energy you use. This can include opting for energy-efficient appliances, reducing single-use plastics, and supporting companies with strong environmental policies.
- **Eco-Anxiety**: Practice mindfulness techniques such as deep breathing, meditation, and grounding exercises to manage stress and anxiety about climate change. These practices help cultivate a calm and balanced state of mind, making it easier to address these issues without becoming overwhelmed.

Chapter 25

Mindfulness and Social Justice

How Can Mindfulness Promote Social Justice?

Mindfulness can serve as a powerful tool in fostering social justice by cultivating empathy, compassion, and interconnectedness. By integrating mindfulness into our social and political lives, we can work towards creating a fairer and more inclusive society.

What is Mindful Listening?

Mindful listening involves actively engaging with others to truly hear and understand their perspectives, especially those of marginalized groups. It requires setting aside judgments and being fully present in the moment. This kind of listening is essential for fostering empathy and understanding, enabling us to respond more compassionately to the experiences and needs of others.

How Can We Develop Empathy and Compassion Through Mindfulness?

Developing empathy and compassion through mindfulness means actively working to alleviate suffering and recognizing our shared humanity. It involves:

- **Practicing Empathy**: Cultivating an understanding of others' feelings and experiences helps build bridges between people and fosters a sense of solidarity.
- **Compassion in Action**: Engaging in acts of kindness and service, guided by mindfulness,

allows us to take tangible steps toward alleviating suffering and promoting justice.

What is Social Justice Mindfulness?

Social justice mindfulness is the practice of meditating on issues of justice and fairness while cultivating a sense of responsibility to address these issues. It involves:

- **Reflecting on Injustice**: Contemplating the root causes of social inequality and considering how we can contribute to meaningful change.
- **Cultivating Responsibility**: Acknowledging our role in societal issues and taking action to promote fairness and equality.

What Does Mindful Activism Entail?

Mindful activism combines the intention of creating positive change with a calm and focused mindset. It's about:

- **Engaging with Intention**: Approaching activism with mindfulness allows us to act with purpose and clarity, rather than reacting impulsively.
- **Non-violent Communication**: Using mindful communication techniques, such as active listening, empathy, and non-violent language, helps resolve conflicts and promotes understanding among diverse groups.
- **Collective Action**: Working together with others in collective efforts, driven by mindfulness,

can lead to meaningful and sustainable social change.

How Can Mindfulness Foster Community Building?

Mindfulness can play a key role in building inclusive and connected communities:

- **Mindful Community Engagement**: By participating in community activities with presence and purpose, individuals can contribute positively to their communities and build stronger, more cohesive groups.
- **Building Bridges**: Connecting with people from diverse backgrounds helps us learn from each other and fosters understanding and unity.
- **Creating Inclusive Spaces**: Ensuring that communities are welcoming and inclusive requires mindfulness in our actions and communication, making it easier for everyone to feel valued and respected.

Why is Creating Inclusive Spaces Important?

Creating inclusive spaces is crucial for promoting social justice as it ensures that everyone feels safe, respected, and valued. This involves:

- **Addressing Barriers**: Identifying and removing barriers that exclude or marginalize certain groups, whether they be physical, social, or cultural.

- **Promoting Equity**: Ensuring equal access and opportunities for all members of the community, regardless of background or identity.

How Does Mindfulness Contribute to a More Just World?

Integrating mindfulness into our social and political lives empowers individuals to contribute to a more just and equitable world:

- **Fostering Justice Through Practice**: By cultivating a mindful awareness of social issues, individuals can contribute more effectively to justice efforts.
- **Empowering Communities**: Mindfulness helps build strong, resilient communities that work together to create positive change.
- **Long-term Impact**: Mindful engagement in social justice issues leads to sustainable change that addresses the root causes of inequality.

Final Thoughts about the Book

As we conclude this journey through the realm of mindfulness, it's important to reflect on the transformative power of this practice. Mindfulness is not just a technique; it's a way of life. It's about cultivating a sense of presence, peace, and purpose in every moment.

Throughout this book, we've explored various aspects of mindfulness, from its historical roots to its contemporary applications. We've delved into the science behind mindfulness, its benefits for mental and physical health, and its potential to transform our relationships, work, and communities.

Remember, the journey of mindfulness is a personal one. There's no right or wrong way to practice mindfulness. The key is to find what works best for you and to be patient with yourself.

Actionable Tips for the Future

To continue your mindfulness journey, consider these actionable tips:

- **Daily Practice:** Set aside time each day for mindfulness practice, even if it's just for a few minutes.
- **Mindful Breathing:** Incorporate mindful breathing into your daily routine.
- **Mindful Movement:** Engage in activities like yoga, tai chi, or mindful walking.
- **Mindful Eating:** Pay attention to the taste, texture, and smell of your food.
- **Mindful Listening:** Actively listen to others without interrupting.
- **Mindful Self-Compassion:** Treat yourself with kindness and understanding.
- **Mindful Technology Use:** Set boundaries on screen time and practice digital mindfulness.
- **Mindful Relationships:** Cultivate strong and meaningful relationships.
- **Mindful Living:** Integrate mindfulness into all aspects of your life.

Final Encouragement

Remember, the journey of mindfulness is a marathon, not a sprint. It's important to be patient with yourself and to celebrate your progress, no matter how small.

Keep exploring new ways to incorporate mindfulness into your life. Attend workshops, retreats, or join a mindfulness group. Share your experiences with others and inspire them to embark on their own mindfulness journey.

By practicing mindfulness, you can unlock your full potential and live a more fulfilling and meaningful life.

Conclusion

In conclusion, mindfulness is a powerful tool that can help you to reduce stress, improve focus, enhance creativity, and cultivate a deeper sense of peace and well-being. By incorporating mindfulness into your daily life, you can transform your relationship with yourself, others, and the world around you.

Remember, the journey of mindfulness is a personal one. There is no right or wrong way to practice. The most important thing is to be patient, kind to yourself, and consistent in your practice.

May your journey of mindfulness be filled with joy, peace, and enlightenment.

++ END ++